At Issue

Sexually
Transmitted Diseases

Other books in the At Issue series:

At Issue

Sexually Transmitted Diseases

Laura Egendorf, Book Editor

GREENHAVEN PRESS

An imprint of Thomson Gale, a part of The Thomson Corporation

Detroit • New York • San Francisco • New Haven, Conn. • Waterville, Maine • London

Christine Nasso, *Publisher*
Elizabeth Des Chenes, *Managing Editor*

© 2007 Thomson Gale, a part of The Thomson Corporation.

Thomson and Star logo are trademarks and Gale and Greenhaven Press are registered trademarks used herein under license.

For more information, contact:
Greenhaven Press
27500 Drake Rd.
Farmington Hills, MI 48331-3535
Or you can visit our Internet site at http://www.gale.com

Articles in Greenhaven Press anthologies are often edited for length to meet page requirements. In addition, original titles of these works are changed to clearly present the main thesis and to explicitly indicate the author's opinion. Every effort is made to ensure that Greenhaven Press accurately reflects the original intent of the authors. Every effort has been made to trace the owners of copyrighted material.

LIBRARY OF CONGRESS CATALOGING-IN-PUBLICATION DATA

Sexually transmitted diseases / Laura Egendorf, book editor.
  p. cm. -- (At issue)
Includes bibliographical references and index.
ISBN-13: 978-0-7377-1975-8 (hardcover)
ISBN-13: 978-0-7377-1976-5 (pbk.)
 1. Sexually transmitted diseases. I. Egendorf, Laura K., 1973-
RA644.V4S36794 2007
616.95'1--dc22

                                        2007005373

ISBN-10: 0-7377-1975-3(hardcover)
ISBN-10: 0-7377-1976-1 (pbk.)

Printed in the United States of America
10 9 8 7 6 5 4 3 2 1

Contents

Introduction

Sexually transmitted diseases are one of the most serious health problems in modern society. Although most people consider the consequences of STDs to be largely physical, these diseases can also affect people economically and socially. Women and children are particularly vulnerable to the impact of STDs, especially those who live in developing nations. If STDs and their related problems are to be reduced, the particular issues facing women and children must be addressed.

STDs, in particular HIV/AIDS, can worsen the economic status of the affected families. When a parent who lives in a developing country dies due to AIDS, especially if his or her family is impoverished, the children are often thrust into the workforce because it is no longer practical or affordable for them to remain in school, and they need to work to make up for the lost income. Such a situation is not uncommon; by 2010 at least 35 million children will have lost one or both parents to AIDS. If the father is the one who has died, his widow may find it difficult to find employment, especially if she did not attend school and lacks employable skills. Many AIDS widows in Africa lose their property and must turn to prostitution to earn a living, a situation that leaves them vulnerable to STDs. As journalist and author Wayne Ellwood contends in *New Internationalist*, "Without property or skills, women are forced to sell their bodies to feed themselves and their children—a dismal choice but one which is more lucrative than the alternative. Poverty means sex workers are more concerned with day-to-day survival than the threat of an infection whose deadly consequences lie many years in the future."

Economic consequences can occur even if the person with an STD is not a parent. Most of the people who die from AIDS are in their prime earning years, the twenties through the forties. As this population dwindles, skilled workers are lost. A country cannot develop economically if its workforce is dying off or becomes too ill to work. Law enforcement and the military are particularly affected—soldiers are two to five times more likely to contract an STD than a person in the general population. The problem worsens when AIDS orphans are unable to go to school and thus cannot find employment as skilled workers when they reach adulthood.

Although AIDS has the most significant economic consequences, other STDs can also have a profound effect. Treating these diseases is a costly strain on health care systems. For example, children with syphilis are hospitalized an average of seven-and-a-half days longer than children without the disease, at a cost of $5,253, according to *Bulletin of the World Health Organization*. A nation that has to spend a disproportionate amount of money on health care has fewer funds to spend on education and infrastructure, which further reduces economic opportunities.

Beyond the economic consequences of STDs are the social repercussions. AIDS death—approximately 2.8 million people died in 2005, including 2 million in sub-Saharan Africa and 560,000 in Southeast Asia—destroys families. AIDS orphans do not experience only an economic loss when a parent dies but a social loss as well, because family bonds are destroyed. Orphaned children, especially girls, are vulnerable to sexual exploitation by older men. If a woman with AIDS in Africa loses her husband due to death or divorce, she can also lose her legal rights. Furthermore, many women with AIDS have been sexually abused, a further sign of their vulnerability both before and after infection.

Alleviating the economic and social consequences of AIDS and other sexually transmitted diseases requires that the rate of infection decline. The best approach may be to improve conditions for the most vulnerable populations. According to *World Health Report 2003*, a publication of the World Health

Organization, "Social and economic rights . . . are central to a future in which HIV will play a less destructive role in people's lives." Governments that provide sexual education, encourage the use of condoms, and empower women so they are not economically dependent on men can make women less vulnerable to sexual exploitation and thus less likely to contract a deadly disease. Increased investment in sexual and reproductive health services may also help reduce the consequences of STDs, such as infertility or children born with AIDS or syphilis. An article in *The Guttmacher Report on Public Policy* states, "Fewer STIs [sexually transmitted infections] means reduced infertility and the stigma associated with it and with HIV/ AIDS. Moreover, at a societal level, the services to support these goals contribute significantly to a range of broader development goals, such as improving the status of women." Not everyone supports such measures, however. For example, many people feel that abstinence is the only viable way to reduce the number of people affected by STDs.

Regardless of which tactics governments and society adopt, sexually transmitted diseases are a problem that the world will likely never completely eradicate. The contributors to *At Issue: Sexually Transmitted Diseases* look at the prevalence of STDs among different populations and debate ways to reduce the spread of these diseases. A perfect solution might never be found, but some approaches may prove especially successful.

1

Sexually Transmitted Diseases in the United States: An Overview

Guttmacher Institute

The Guttmacher Institute is an organization that conducts research and analysis on sexual and reproductive health.

Sexually transmitted diseases are a problem that affects millions of Americans and costs the nation $13 billion per year. Some of the most prevalent STDs are the human papillomavirus (HPV), which infects 6.2 million Americans each year, and chlamydia, which was diagnosed 929,462 times in 2004. Each year 40,000 Americans are infected with the most serious STD, HIV/AIDS. STDs are disproportionately prevalent among African Americans and teenagers.

Facts on Sexually Transmitted Infections in the United States

- STIs [sexually transmitted infections] are not new; even HIV, the most recently recognized infection, has been around for more than two decades. Many STIs or their manifestations have been recognized for centuries.

- STIs are caused by bacterial, viral or parasitic pathogens that are acquired through sexual activity.

- At one end of the spectrum is HIV/AIDS, which is considered to be fatal but is treatable with antiretroviral

Guttmacher Institute, "Facts on Sexually Transmitted Infections in the United States," *Facts in Brief*, August 2006. Reproduced by permission of Alan Guttmacher Institute.

drugs and can extend an infected individual's life by years. Other viral STIs, such as hepatitis B and herpes, are also incurable, but are treatable with much less medical care required and fewer side effects.

- At the other end of the spectrum are many of the most common STIs—bacterial infections, such as chlamydia, gonorrhea and syphilis—which are treatable and curable.

- Left untreated, chlamydia and gonorrhea may lead to serious complications, including infertility and chronic pain; syphilis may result in death. In addition, some STIs increase a person's vulnerability to getting HIV.

- Many STIs are "silent," in that they cause few symptoms. Without symptoms, many STIs can be diagnosed only through testing, yet routine screening is not widespread.

Measuring the Prevalence of STIs

- Data collection may be incomplete because some STIs (such as herpes and HIV) are not part of a national reporting system, because some STIs (such as chlamydia and HPV [human papillomavirus]) can be asymptomatic and go undetected, and because surveys intended to measure the prevalence of STIs have not been based on representative samples of the U.S. population.

- It is difficult to measure trends in the incidence and prevalence of STIs because of changes in reporting systems and the availability of increasingly accurate testing methods.

- Only chlamydia, gonorrhea, syphilis, hepatitis A and hepatitis B are required to be reported to state health departments and the U.S. Centers for Disease Control and Prevention (CDC).

- In 2004, the CDC reported 929,462 chlamydia diagnoses and 330,132 gonorrhea diagnoses. However, since most chlamydia and gonorrhea cases go undiagnosed or are not reported, the true number of new infections is probably much greater.

- In 2004, the most infectious stages of syphilis—primary and secondary—were diagnosed in nearly 8,000 Americans, and hepatitis B virus (HBV) infections in 60,000. An estimated 1.25 million people in the United States have chronic HBV.

- Although other STIs are not required to be reported to the CDC, estimates are available for some. The CDC estimates that one out of five adolescents and adults have had a genital herpes infection, and 7.4 million new cases of trichomoniasis occur each year.

- The CDC also estimates that 20 million people are currently infected with HPV, 6.2 million Americans get a new HPV infection each year and at least 50% of sexually active individuals will acquire an HPV infection at some point in their lives. Most HPV infections cause no clinical problems and resolve on their own without treatment. (As many as 91% of new infections clear up within two years.) Some strains of HPV may lead to persistent infection that can progress to cervical cancer if left untreated, however this outcome is largely preventable with effective screening.

HIV/AIDS in the United States

- Since 1981, when the first cases of AIDS were identified, 1.4 million Americans have been infected with HIV, including more than 500,000 who have already died. Roughly 40,000 new HIV infections occur each year—a number that has remained stable since the early 1990s.

- An estimated 1–1.2 million U.S. individuals are living with HIV. As many as one in four individuals with HIV may be unaware of their status.

- One-half of men and women aged 15–44 report that they have been tested at least once (other than through blood donation); 15% in the past 12 months.

- In 2004, women accounted for 27% of HIV/AIDS diagnoses among adolescents and adults, and males for 73%. However, this gap is slowly closing.

- Heterosexual transmission accounts for a large proportion of newly diagnosed HIV cases among women. Seventy-six percent of women in whom HIV was diagnosed between 2001 and 2004 contracted the virus through heterosexual intercourse.

Gender and Racial Differences

- In 2004, the overall rate of chlamydia infection among women (485 cases per 100,000 females) was more than three times the rate among men (147 per 100,000).

- The rate of chlamydia among black women (1,722 per 100,000) was nearly eight times the rate among white women (227 per 100,000). The rate among black men (645 per 100,000) was more than 11 times that of white men (57.3 per 100,000).

- Blacks remain the group most heavily affected by gonorrhea. In 2004, the gonorrhea rate among blacks was 19 times the rate among whites.

- Although blacks make up only approximately 13% of the U.S. population, they accounted for one-half of the estimated new HIV/AIDS diagnoses in 2004.

STIs Among Teens and Young Adults

- Although teens and young adults represent only 25% of the sexually active population, 15–24-year-olds account for nearly half of all STI diagnoses each year.

- Rates of gonorrhea, chlamydia and syphilis are above average among young people.

- Together, HPV, trichomoniasis and chlamydia represent nearly nine in 10 new STIs among 15–24-year-olds.

Prevention, Treatment, and Cost

- The three ways to avoid STIs are to abstain from sex, to be in a long-term, mutually monogamous relationship with a partner who has been tested and does not have an STI, and to use condoms consistently and correctly.

- Male latex condoms have been proven effective in preventing the most serious STI (HIV), the most easily transmitted STIs (gonorrhea, chlamydia and HPV) and unplanned pregnancy. However, no protective method is 100% effective, and condom use cannot guarantee absolute protection against any STI.

- Access to health care services, including STI screening and treatment, is critical, because not all STIs can be prevented, even with perfect condom use, and because so many STIs are asymptomatic and can cause long-term health risks if undetected and untreated.

- Direct medical costs associated with STIs in the United States are estimated at $13 billion annually.

- More than $8 billion is spent each year to diagnose and treat STIs and their complications. This figure does not include HIV.

2

Sexually Transmitted Diseases Are a Moral Problem

Karen Testerman

Karen Testerman is the executive director of Cornerstone Policy Research, a conservative public policy organization.

Americans' lax sexual values have led to the growing problem of sexually transmitted diseases. Adolescents are taught that sex outside of marriage and homosexuality are acceptable, despite the fact that these behaviors are associated with STDs such as AIDS, herpes, and gonorrhea. STDs are not only a moral problem; they also lead to cancer and sterility. The best way to end the problem of STDs is to teach children that they should save sexual intercourse for marriage and never engage in heterosexual or homosexual promiscuity.

We are facing a plague of massive proportions, a plague made more sinister because it attacks not only adults but our youth. What is this crisis? It is a pandemic of sexually transmitted diseases (STDs) that is encouraged by a message of "safe sex" and an adult population that acts as if self-control and traditional morality are outdated and without value.

Society focuses on the increase in out-of-wedlock and teen births. Meanwhile STDs tear through our youth and adult population at alarming and deadly rates. Pregnancy is seldom fatal (except for aborted babies), but the STDs of today are. They are "not your father's" STDs, which were few and easily cured with penicillin.

In the 1960s, syphilis and gonorrhea were the two most prevalent STDs; today, there are more than 20 and some have as many as 80–100 strains. Despite the fitting publicity that the deadly epidemic of human immunodeficiency virus/ acquired immune disorder syndrome (HIV/AIDS) commands, according to research at the University of New Mexico, human papilloma virus (HPV), not HIV, is the most common STD transmitted today.

What is the magnitude of the problem? According to recent testimony before the House Committee on Energy and Commerce, "Three to four million STDs are contracted yearly by 15- to 19-year-olds, and another five to six million STDs are contracted annually by 20- to 24-year-olds."

Children Learn a Fatal Message

Perhaps the most tragic aspect of this plague is the role adults play in it. Failures by grown-ups are the primary cause of the pandemic among our youth. Adults are failing our children by promoting a fatal message about sex: both in education and in actions. Youth are allowed to believe that there is such a thing as safe sex outside of marriage and that any sexual practice is acceptable as long as the participants are smiling.

Billboards, TV, magazines, movies, and catalogs promote the message that sex is the way to be cool, to fit in, to solve life's challenges. Today, the initial onset of sexual activity is occurring at younger ages, while couples delay the decision to marry or prefer cohabitation. Dr. Meg Meeker, a pediatrician and author of *Epidemic: How Teen Sex Is Killing Our Kids*, reports that half of all students in the ninth through twelfth grades have had sexual intercourse. Additionally, the average age for the onset of puberty in girls has dropped from 12 to 10.

There are physical and emotional consequences of engaging in sexual activity outside of marriage. Unwed childbearing costs American taxpayers $29 billion a year in social services, lost tax revenue, and the consequences of delinquency and poverty among teenage parents. These teens will enter adulthood disadvantaged and will convey this disadvantage to their children.

A girl is four times more likely to contract an STD than she is to become pregnant.

In 1960, 15 percent of teen births in the United States were out-of-wedlock. More recently, despite the reduction in teen pregnancy, the out-of-wedlock birthrate was 78 percent among teens, according to the National Center for Health Statistics (2000).

Problems Associated with Single-Parent Households

Meanwhile, the No. 1 indicator of poverty in our nation is single-parent households among 15- to 19-year-olds. Ninety percent of these young people will never attend college. Eighty percent of women who choose to parent while they are teens will live at the poverty level for 10 years or more.

Linda Waite, professor of urban sociology at the University of Chicago, and Maggie Gallagher, affiliate scholar at the Institute for American Values, have found that children born to unmarried mothers are more likely to die in infancy. Boys raised in single-parent homes are twice as likely to commit a crime that leads to incarceration by their early thirties.

Adolescents raised by single parents or stepfamilies are more likely to engage in sexual intercourse and to be sexually active at an earlier age, according to Dawn M. Upchurch, professor at the UCLA School of Public Health. None of this takes into account the impact of postabortive trauma or the emotional trauma of making tough decisions to allow adoption so that the child will have better opportunities.

The data are stark, but the true disaster is the damage wreaked by STDs. A girl is four times more likely to contract an STD than she is to become pregnant. Today, it is likely a young mother has on average 2.3 STDs. Syphilis, gonorrhea, herpes, chlamydia, hepatitis A and B, HIV, and HPV are the most common. Many of the viral STDs have multiple strains.

A leading risk factor is the number of sexual partners. Vital health statistics directly link this factor to the early onset of sexual activity. Consider the teen who has sex with 6 people, each of whom has 6 partners. According to Dr. Meeker, this means that 36 people have been exposed to disease.

The Dangers of Homosexual Intercourse

Marcel T. Saghir, coauthor of *Male and Female Homosexuality: A Comprehensive Investigation*, cites the magnification of this problem in the homosexual community, even among those who define themselves as monogamous. The average such relationship among homosexual males lasts less than three years. Despite attempts to portray their choice for living as normal and healthy, homosexuals are in the highest risk group for several of the most serious STDs.

Evidence from the National Cancer Institute that smoking shortens a person's life by 7–10 years led to a multibillion-dollar lawsuit by state governments. However, despite numerous studies that reveal homosexual relationships can reduce male or female lives by 10–30 years, tolerance and political correctness reign.

As even homosexual supporters and the media admit, the increasing pressure to accept homosexual practices as mainstream is dramatically affecting our society. According to the *New York Blade News Reports*, gay men are in the highest-risk group for several of the most serious diseases, including STDs.

Instability and promiscuity are characteristic of homosexual relationships. Even the Gay Lesbian Medical Association agrees with mainstream reports that, despite decades of intensive efforts to educate, HIV/AIDS continues to increase among the homosexual community.

According to another homosexual newspaper, the *Washington Blade*, HPV is "almost universal" among homosexuals. HPV, often asymptomatic, is believed to be the causative vector of cervical cancer in women. It can also lead to anal cancer in men.

Add to this the confusion about what constitutes sexual activity. Is it just penile penetration of the vagina? Does oral sex count? Is heavy petting to be included? What about practices of homosexuals? Common wisdom seems to promote the idea that these questions are irrelevant, as a condom can prevent the passing of bodily fluids, and thus HIV/AIDS.

The Threat of HPV and Chlamydia

Sadly, this misconception leads to even more danger, as the passing of body fluids is not the only way to contract these diseases. Even a properly used and defect-free latex condom will not completely protect against all STDs. Any genital contact can cause an infection! Genital warts are the common name for HPV. The most common and contagious of STDs, HPV is passed by skin-to-skin contact. It is the leading cause of cervical cancer and in its cancerous form does not exhibit any symptoms.

Alas, most of our sexually active, infected youth do not know they have a disease. Some viruses can lie dormant in the body for up to 30 years before symptoms develop. Ninety percent of those infected with chlamydia exhibit no symptoms and receive no treatment.

According to abstinence speaker Pam Stenzel, the statistics of this disaster are staggering, especially among our youth. Every day in America, 12,000 teenagers contract a sexually transmitted disease. How many is an acceptable loss?

The American Medical Association recommends that sexually active girls be tested for chlamydia every six months. Why just girls? Aren't boys infected as well? Yes, men carry the infection, but as is often the case, girls endure most of the consequences. Stenzel points out that the female reproductive system is open; scar tissue builds up on the cervix, fallopian tubes, and ovaries as a result of pelvic inflammatory disease (PID) from the chlamydia infection.

With a single chlamydia infection, there is a 25 percent chance of sterility. With a second infection there is a 50 percent chance of sterility. If there is a third infection, it is almost certain that the girl will be sterile—all due to PID.

This is why, some people reason, we should promote a dual message and sell teens on abstinence with "safe sex" as a backup. The dual message approach says that abstinence is best, but if you choose to engage in genital contact, use some form of contraception, usually condoms. This comprehensive message indicates that our youth are no more than bundles of uncontrollable hormones—that they are no more than mere animals. Many public school sexuality education programs instruct youth in the proper use of condoms and contraception. The information given is that condoms significantly reduce the chance of STD infection.

Promiscuous sexual practices, whether heterosexual or homosexual, are highly costly to Americans.

In reality, even if a condom is used 100 percent of the time, a sexually active young person is at risk to contract STDs including gonorrhea, chlamydia, and trichomoniasis. Even when used, a condom fails to prevent pregnancy 12 percent of the time, according to the Maryland Center for Mental and Child Health. Despite faithful use of the condom, the person who engages in genital contact is not immune from contracting an STD that spreads through skin-to-skin contact.

It is time that adults cleaned up their act and encouraged youth to aspire to achieve the goal of being responsible, thinking people. Young people need adults who will trust them enough to give them the information they need to make good choices.

Sex Outside of Marriage Is Harmful

Young people need to know that sex without boundaries is deadly. There are consequences when engaging in genital contact outside the bonds of marriage. Young people need to know that both parties should wait until they make a lifelong commitment to one another in marriage to have sex. Within marriage, they have a better chance to be healthier, to attain a higher level of education, to be financially secure, to be happier and enjoy sex more, but only if that sex is with their marital partner.

The only way to protect against STDs that can have lifelong, physically and emotionally painful consequences is to abstain from genital contact outside of marriage. According to the University of Chicago research in Sex in America, researchers report that when a marriage is intact, the couple almost never have sex outside their marital relationship.

Promiscuous sexual practices, whether heterosexual or homosexual, are highly costly to Americans. The health of present and future generations is in jeopardy. The idea that avoiding pregnancy or homosexual behavior is enough is dangerous. This attitude completely ignores the possibility and consequences of exposure to STDs. Add to this the disease of substance abuse and emotional trauma due to abortion, depression, anxiety, and subsequent problems, and it is clear that one should avoid promiscuity at all costs.

Despite the rhetoric, everyone is not doing it! Over 50 percent of our youth are not engaging in genital contact with one another. Given the information, our young people are capable of making informed decisions. Once we realize this, we can give them (and society) a future without this plague.

The promiscuous plague has many facets. Messages in the media, peer pressure, alcohol, and drugs all influence teen sexual behavior. The biggest influences, of course, are parents. The actions of young people reflect what adults transmit. This is done through how adults behave and what is communicated as acceptable. By allowing the media to undermine morality, the plague is fostered. By engaging in dangerous sexual practices, the plague is encouraged.

More important, by abdicating parental responsibility, the plague is promoted. A recent survey of teens conducted by L.B. Whitbeck, professor of sociology at the University of Nebraska, found that parents have the strongest effect on a teen's decision whether to have sex. Parents influence the attitude of their teens by their own marital status, their attitudes, the amount of supervision they provide, and how involved they are with their children.

Ultimately, the most effective inoculation against this plague is effective parenting. Certainly parenting would be made easier if the entertainment media reduced their hard sell of "anything goes" sex and schools truly taught nonmarital abstinence and credited our youth with the ability to use good sense. If given the opportunity, teens can and will make good choices. Our next generation needs to know it is okay to say no!

3

Sexually Transmitted Diseases Are an International Public Health Crisis

Gina A. Dallabetta, Mary Lyn Field, Marie Laga, and Q. Monir Islam

Gina A. Dallabetta is an associate director for the AIDS Control and Prevention Project. Mary Lyn Field is the director of the John Snow Inc. HIV/AIDS programs. Marie Laga is the head of epidemiology and interventions at the Institute of Tropical Medicine in Belgium. Q. Monir Islam is a doctor at the World Health Organization.

Sexually transmitted diseases are an international problem with serious health, social, and economic consequences, particularly in developing countries. People who are infected with STDs such as gonorrhea and chlamydia are also more likely to transmit the HIV virus. STDs lead to a number of health problems, including infertility and maternal mortality. These diseases also create social and economic problems, especially for infected women who are stigmatized and rejected by their husbands and families.

Although sexually transmitted diseases (STDs) have been causing significant morbidity and mortality for years, it is only with the advent of the human immunodeficiency virus (HIV) that STD control is now receiving higher priority in both developed and developing countries. This is because

Gina A. Dallabetta, Mary Lyn Field, Marie Laga, and Q. Monir Islam, *Control of Sexually Transmitted Diseases: A Handbook for the Design and Management of Programs.* Research Triangle Park, NC: AIDSCAP/Family Health International, 2006. © The AIDSCAP Electronic Library (Family Health International/The AIDS Control and Prevention Project (AIDSCAP), Durham, North Carolina). Reproduced by permission.

STDs increase the transmission of HIV and have similar behavioral risk factors. Globally, it is estimated that as many as 333 million new cases of curable STDs occur each year. The indisputable facts that STDs produce serious economic, social and health consequences, made more clear by their association with HIV, and that all STDs are preventable and many are curable, make it incumbent on governments, communities and donors to meet the challenge of STD prevention and control.

Modeling the dynamic effect of STD prevention or cure on subsequent HIV and STD rates illustrates a dramatic effect. By curing or preventing one hundred cases of syphilis among an STD high-risk (core) group, approximately 109 new HIV infections and 4,132 new syphilis cases could be prevented in the next ten years. The prospect that the consequences of STDs, including HIV infection, can be prevented, is a hopeful one.

[According to M. Over and P. Piot,] "It is truly remarkable that this high rank [of STDs] in terms of both burden and potential health gain is not reflected in higher specific expenditure for the control of HIV infection and CSTDs (classic STDs). Neglected training, poor diagnostic and therapeutic capabilities, high rates of quasi-irreversible sequelae [afteraffects] and insufficient research and development efforts (at least for classic STDs) are all symptoms of this inadequate response."

The Challenges Posed by STDs

This [viewpoint] explores the epidemiology of STDs, and the epidemic's health and socioeconomic consequences in developing countries. It also looks at the challenges which, if met, could mitigate the impact of STDs. The challenges are considerable. In many countries, the health-care systems are already strained dealing with other health problems. STDs, as they are classically diagnosed and treated, demand a level of provider time and diagnostic facilities that many countries do not possess. The stigma associated with STDs, the limited resources and limited access to suitable health care for those most at risk (women and youth), and the lack of affordable and effective drugs are just some of the constraints to STD control. There are also constraints within countries served by STD programs. For example, many beliefs and practices about STDs interfere with effective treatment. . . .

For several decades, STDs have ranked among the top five categories for which adults in developing countries seek health-care services.

Numerous epidemiologic and biologic studies now support the fact that STDs, both ulcerative and non-ulcerative, enhance HIV transmission. In addition, it appears that HIV alters the natural history of some STDs. HIV has been identified in the genital tract of both males and females and found to be both cell-associated and cell-free. HIV has also been isolated from the exudates of both male and female genital ulcers. The shedding of HIV in genital fluids is increased by STD-related inflammatory responses and exudates from lesions, making men and women who are STD-infected and HIV-positive more infective. Furthermore, it has been found that when women have gonorrhea or chlamydial infection there is a disproportionate increase in CD4 lymphocytes, the HIV target cell, in the endocervix. Studies have shown that treating STDs reduces the percentage of men in whom HIV is detected and the amount of HIV in ejaculate. In a recent community-based, randomized trial in the Mwanza district of rural Tanzania, treating STD-symptomatic individuals using the syndromic approach reduced HIV incidence in the study population by 42 percent.

For several decades, STDs have ranked among the top five categories for which adults in developing countries seek health-care services. Although in Northern and Western Europe there has been a spectacular decline in the incidence of STDs, particularly gonorrhea and syphilis, the situation in North America is more variable with increases continuing in inner-city minority populations. In developing countries both the prevalence and incidence of STDs are still very high, with STDs making up the second cause of healthy life lost in women of 15 to 45 years of age after maternal morbidity and mortality. In men, if HIV and other STDs are combined, sexually transmitted infections account for nearly 15 percent of all healthy life lost in this age group. . . .

STDs have effects that extend far beyond the individual's physical or psychological discomfort.

The Health, Social, and Economic Consequences of STDs

STDs have effects that extend far beyond the individual's physical or psychological discomfort. The greatest impact of STDs is on women and children. In women between 15 and 44 years of age, the morbidity and mortality due to STDs, not including HIV, are second only to maternal causes. The prevalence of curable STDs in women is highly variable by region and risk behavior. . . .

Of note is that the majority of curable STDs in women cause subclinical or asymptomatic infection. For example, gonorrhea usually causes symptoms in men, allowing them to seek treatment, whereas women are frequently either asymptomatic or have minor symptoms. There are limited diagnostics available in developing countries for routine screening of asymptomatic women or even for testing of symptomatic women.

In many parts of the developing world, pelvic inflammatory disease (PID) is the most common reason for admission to gynecological wards. PID sequelae [aftereffects] include infertility, ectopic pregnancy with subsequent maternal mortality, chronic pelvic pain, an increased risk of subsequent pelvic infections and a higher risk of hysterectomy. Infertility as a result of PID accounts for 50 to 80 percent of the infertility in Africa: in Latin America, about 35 percent. In cultures in which childbearing holds very high value, infertility as a consequence of gonococcal or chlamydial infection is tragic. . . .

Treponema pallidum, the cause of syphilis, can cross the placental barrier and infect the fetus. *Neisseria gonorrhoeae* and *Chlamydia trachomatis* also cause morbidity in the mother and neonate. . . .

An STD brings emotional consequences for those involved, including depression and its medical and social effects.

In addition to the health complications of STDs, it is also important to look at the painful social consequences of untreated STDs suffered primarily by women in the developing world. For many, social stigma and personal damage due to infertility and pregnancy wastage result in divorce or commercial sex work. And in Tanzania, a husband can return an infertile woman to her parents. In addition, the husband may request the return of her bride price.

The complex interaction of infertility and other social factors in African society is depicted as follows:

Marital instability caused by infertility and the spread of venereal disease caused by marital instability and sexual mobility can form a vicious cycle. The movement of abandoned or rejected barren women to urban prostitution has been noted in Niger, Uganda, and the Central African Republic. Similarly, in many of these societies, marital and sexual mobility on the part of the women is interpreted as a desperate attempt to become pregnant, and tolerance on the part of society as a means to maximize their chances of doing so. . . . Once venereal disease was introduced into a community with some degree of sexual or marital mobility, its diffusion might have been assured by the existing customs. [Subsequently] the mobility itself [may have been] intensified to overcome the fertility effects.

In addition to the impact of infertility, significant conflicts arise between couples, their families who become aware, and friends who are part of their support system. There is also the psychological and emotional burden of trust that is undermined, and the subsequent energy expended by partners to resume harmonious relationships. The number of incidents of violence and abusive behavior or retribution as a result of discovering an STD probably remains undocumented. What can be understood from experience is that an STD brings emotional consequences for those involved, including depression and its medical and social effects.

Studies documenting the economic consequences of STDs are limited. The costs of pelvic inflammatory disease in the U.S. have been estimated to reach 3.5 billion dollars. It also has been estimated that 5 percent of the total discounted healthy life years lost in sub-Saharan Africa is due to STDs, excluding HIV. HIV alone accounts for 10 percent of healthy life years lost. More studies have been conducted recently that address the economic consequences of HIV.

4

HIV Infections Among African American Women Is a Serious Problem

Jon Cohen

Jon Cohen writes for Science *magazine.*

HIV and AIDS have disproportionately affected African-American women. Although African Americans are only 13 percent of the population, 72 percent of all American women who are infected with HIV are African American. Several theories have been suggested to explain why that population is high risk. One possibility is the link between poverty and HIV infections. Another explanation is that some African American men secretly engage in homosexual activity, become infected, and then infect their female partners. A third theory is that the incarceration of African American men has led to both men and women having an increased number of sexual partners, making it easier for HIV to spread within the population. American politicians must stop ignoring the problem.

When [journalist] Gwen Ifill asked a pressing question about AIDS during the [2004] vice-presidential debate, both candidates were utterly lost. "I want to talk to you about AIDS, and not about AIDS in China or Africa, but AIDS right here in this country, where black women between the ages of 25 and 44 are 13 times more likely to die of the disease than their counterparts," said Ifill. "What should the government's role be in helping to end the growth of this epidemic?"

Jon Cohen, "A Silent Epidemic: Why Is There Such a High Percentage of HIV and AIDS Among Black Women?" *Slate*, October 27, 2004. Reproduced by permission of the author.

[Dick] Cheney did not bother trying to hide his ignorance. "I have not heard those numbers with respect to African-American women. I was not aware that it was—that they're in epidemic there [sic]," he said. [John] Edwards resorted to dodge ball, spending his 90 seconds on AIDS in Africa, the genocide in Sudan, uninsured Americans, and John Kerry. "OK, we'll move on," said Ifill, who somehow restrained herself from rolling her eyes à la Jon Stewart.

Cheney and Edwards both suffered sharp criticism for their shockingly vacuous replies—a competent briefing on HIV/AIDS in the United States could have made these men at least conversant on the topic in less time than it takes them to do their on-air hair and makeup. Besides, in debates, even a shallow answer scores more points than saying "I dunno" or changing the subject.

The Extent of the Problem

That said, coming up with a *sophisticated* answer to Ifill's question is a tall order. AIDS researchers don't have a solid explanation for why black women in America have such a shockingly high prevalence of HIV infection and AIDS, which makes it difficult to spell out precisely how the government should respond to the problem—other than to reach out to these women more aggressively and to conduct more studies.

Black women in 2002 accounted for 67 percent of the country's AIDS cases among women.

The data that investigators do have makes it clear that heterosexual sex is the primary mode of transmission, accounting for 74 percent of the HIV/AIDS cases reported in 2002 in black American women. Yet attempts to tease out the dynamics that drive this heterosexual spread have led to more theories than hard facts, with researchers using such different methods to gather their data that it's hard to compare their results. One particularly splashy speculation also has attracted more of the spotlight than it deserves: black men "on the down low," who identify themselves as heterosexual but secretly have sex with men.

Without question, there is a higher percentage of HIV and AIDS in the black female population in the United States. The Centers for Disease Control and Prevention last year looked at data from 1999 to 2002 reported by 29 states that track HIV infections. The data are somewhat skewed because several states that have serious AIDS problems—including California, New York, and Illinois—did not at that time tally HIV infections. Still, the study found that black women accounted for nearly 72 percent of the female cases, while whites made up 18 percent and Hispanics 8.5 percent. Given that only 13 percent of Americans are black, you don't need a statistician to see the scale of the problem. (Encouragingly, the number of new HIV cases reported in women, regardless of race, did not increase during the four years that the study analyzed.)

When looking at people whose HIV infection progresses to the point of causing AIDS, the disproportionate toll on black women becomes clearer still. Black women in 2002 accounted for 67 percent of the country's AIDS cases among women. For the sake of comparison, consider that blacks had a rate of 48 cases per 100,000 blacks, while whites had a rate of 2 per 100,000 whites. There's an interesting geographic distribution of cases, too, that may offer important clues about forces propelling this particular epidemic: The vast majority of black women with AIDS live in the South and the Northeast. The CDC's HIV/AIDS statistics do not offer a breakdown of income and healthcare insurance, but that's an obvious place to look for explanations.

Ifill's question referred specifically to AIDS deaths in 25-to-44 year olds. The figure she cited actually took many AIDS researchers by surprise but seems to have come from the National Vital Statistics report issued last year that shows black women in 2001 had a rate of death from AIDS 14 times (not 13 times) higher than that of whites.

Theories Behind the Numbers

Why does such a problem exist? No compelling evidence suggests that blacks have any special genetic susceptibility to HIV. The CDC offers a laundry list of reasons of why African American men and women have relatively high rates of HIV infection and AIDS. The two most convincing explanations on the list: poverty and sexually transmitted diseases. The 2000 U.S. Census found that one in four blacks lived in poverty, and studies clearly have shown a strong link between poverty and the risk of HIV infection. Poor people also receive lower-quality healthcare, which means they will often progress from HIV infection to AIDS more quickly. And the link to sexually transmitted diseases, which create open sores that facilitate the spread of HIV, is equally clear-cut: Blacks are 24 times more likely to contract gonorrhea and eight times more likely to get syphilis.

The CDC list also includes community denial about injection drug use and homosexuality, but there is scant evidence to support the notion that those risk factors are somehow higher in blacks. In fact, injection drug use, a particularly effective way to spread HIV, is actually *lower* in black women than in white women: It accounted for 24 percent of HIV/AIDS cases among black females in 2002 and 34 percent among white females. It could be that black women are having sex with more men who are injecting drugs, but no compelling data back that conclusion, either.

Then there's the much ballyhooed "down low" phenomenon. Some men on the DL are becoming infected by anal intercourse with men and then spreading the infection to their female partners, a transmission route that became widely discussed [in 2004] with the publication of J.L. King's *On the Down Low: A Journey Into the Lives of "Straight" Black Men*

Who Sleep With Men. But the great unknown is how frequently this occurs, and whether it's truly different in blacks versus whites or Hispanics.

The Role of African American Men

Because of a flurry of media coverage about the DL link, including an *Oprah* show featuring King and a *New York Times Magazine* story, many who study AIDS in the black community cringe at its mention. "I'm sick of hearing about it," says Victoria Cargill, an epidemiologist at the Office of AIDS Research at the National Institutes of Health. Cargill, who also works at a clinic in poor, black Southeast D.C., says the high prevalence of HIV/AIDS in women can clearly be attributed to a host of factors that have nothing to do with the DL. "I'm not saying it doesn't exist, but if we start adding up how many people this affects, this is the eye of the needle," says Cargill. "Let's start talking about the needle." CDC epidemiologist Greg Millett says that when it comes to the DL phenomenon, there simply are more questions than answers. "The truth is there are very few studies that deal with bisexual black men and even fewer that deal with the down low," says Millett, who has put together a provocative PowerPoint presentation on the topic.

The single biggest driver of the heterosexual spread [of AIDS] to black women is the incarceration of black men.

A fascinating CDC study published [in 2003] specifically looked at men who have sex with men and do not disclose their sexual orientation versus those who do disclose. The study recruited participants from only six gay bars (which already tilts the results away from DL men who may not go to gay bars), but the findings were startling. More black men were nondisclosers (18 percent)—that is, on the DL—than white men (8 percent), and all nondisclosures reported having more sex with women than with men. But nondisclosers of all races were also less likely to be infected with HIV than disclosers, and black nondisclosers in particular reported significantly less unprotected anal intercourse with men than did black disclosers. Several other recent studies have found higher proportions of bisexual black men than white men, but it's unclear whether how much of an HIV "bridge" they are to black women.

Phill Wilson, executive director of the Black AIDS Institute in Los Angeles, suggests, rather, that the single biggest driver of the heterosexual spread to black women is the incarceration of black men. "The prison industry in America is an almost exact replication of the mining industry in South Africa, where you take large groups of men and move them from their families for an extended period of time," says Wilson. As studies conducted in South Africa have shown, men who leave their homes for the mines often have new sexual partners—as do the women they leave behind. The increased sexual mixing spreads HIV in both the migrant men and their regular partners. When they return home, the men may infect their regular partners—or vice versa. This pattern of sexual networking is called concurrent partnering, which means that relationships overlap, and there's nothing that HIV likes more.

Wilson and others argue that with so many men cycling in and out of the African American community, women end up at a greater risk because of similar disruptions of sexual networks and the resultant concurrency patterns: They mix with new partners when their men leave and often reunite with them when they are released. Incarceration also exposes many men to anal sex, whether by coercion or choice, and injection-drug use, the two most efficient ways to spread HIV. And if the locked-up man was the main wage earner, poverty can be a factor, too.

One superb study of concurrency in African Americans in rural North Carolina found that 53 percent of the men and 31 percent of the women reported concurrent partners during the preceding five years. Interestingly, 80 percent of the men in the study who said they had been incarcerated for more than 24 hours reported having had concurrent partners within five years; that percentage plummeted to 43 percent if a man had not been locked up for a day or longer.

Equally important, black women have a small pool of black men to choose from at any given time. "African American women are the only group in the United States where there are fewer men than women," says Gail Wyatt, an associate director of the AIDS Institute at the University of California, Los Angeles. "The availability of a partner who shares the same values is much less likely. The women are more likely to be educated than their partners. They're more likely to be employed." As a result of the shortage of black men, black women are vulnerable to becoming involved with men who are engaging in risky behaviors that they don't know about, whether it be having unprotected sex with other partners, female or male; visiting sex workers; or injecting drugs.

The muddy truth is that the high rate of HIV infection and AIDS among African American women is due to a combination of all these factors. "It's a perfect storm of issues," says NIH's Cargill.

An Ignored Population

And there's one more factor to consider, says Wilson: Politicians ignore this population. "It's both a cause and a symptom of the problem that our government really is not interested in the health and well-being of black people and in particular black women," says Wilson. "How is it that Dick Cheney can tell you how many machine guns are in Baghdad, but doesn't have a clue about issues that are killing black women a stone's throw from his office?"

Gwen Ifill, for her part, received so many queries about this particular question that she wrote out a response, refreshingly candid, that her publicist gave out to people who inquired. "I have to say I was surprised that neither the Vice President nor the Senator had an answer on this," wrote Ifill. "As a black woman, I also found it depressing. The good news is that, in the feedback I have gotten since the debate, folks got that. These debates have been very useful for smart and involved likely voters. They have gotten to see what these folks do, and don't, care about."

5

Methamphetamine Use Is Increasing the Spread of HIV

David Boddiger

David Boddiger is a writer for Lancet, *a medical journal.*

The growing popularity of Metamphetamine [British spelling] within the homosexual community has worsened the problem of AIDS. Because Metamphetamine removes inhibitions, its users are more likely to engage in unprotected sex. In addition, Metamphetamine users who inject the drug are at greater risk of contracting AIDS. Metamphetamine users also have difficulty following their AIDS treatment regimens. However, metamphetamine's popularity among homosexual men should not be considered the only factor in the spread of HIV and AIDS.

A few years ago, Daniel Berger, medical director of Northstar Healthcare, Chicago's largest private HIV clinic, began noticing worrying changes in his patients. Despite being on what should have been effective treatment, a number of his patients were developing unexpected health problems. Some were losing weight, but did not seem to have AIDS. Some, even young patients, were developing hypertension and cardiomyopathy.

And there were also signs that they were engaging in unsafe sexual practices, with a spike in the number of patients contracting syphilis and hepatitis C. Several patients were developing social problems, such as losing their jobs. Berger even noticed an increase in the number of patients failing to keep their appointments. When a patient died of a metamphetamine[British spelling]-induced heart attack, Berger began to suspect that many of the problems he was seeing were due to metamphetamine use by his patients.

Methamphetamine Use Is Spreading

Keith, a 41-year-old gay man who asked that his last name not be used, was one of those patients. Keith had contracted HIV in 1986 and had responded well to antiretroviral therapy. But he watched dozens of his friends die of AIDS and eventually he started using metamphetamine in 1999 to escape depression. "Crystal popped me right out of it", he says.

Within a year he was a daily user, going through a half-gram of "crystal" daily, he says. "I lost my house, friends, and family, I had no money, but I didn't care, it seemed normal."

He also began to engage in high-risk sex. Before he started using metamphetamine Keith says he had sex with one or two partners a month. After he started using, he says it was normal to have sex with at least 20 partners a week. "It was one sexual encounter after another", he says.

He kept this up for 1.5 years. Then he had a series of heart attacks, which Berger believes were induced by metamphetamine.

Health and law enforcement officials in the USA are becoming increasingly alarmed over the rapid spread of metamphetamine use—known on the street as meth, crystal, speed, or ice. But health officials are especially concerned about what they say is a new epidemic of HIV transmission among urban gay men—an epidemic they say is linked in part to the rise of metamphetamine use within the gay community. Long a problem on the west coast, in recent years metamphetamine has spread into the Midwest as well, including Chicago.

For many, snorting, smoking, and injecting metamphet-amine—which is cheaper and more addictive than heroin—helps ease psychological stress associated with HIV infection. However, as the drug wears off, users plummet into depression and often become suicidal. Like Keith, many addicts continue using on a regular basis to avoid the psychological pitfalls of withdrawal.

Other "club drugs" are used with crystal, including MDMA (Ecstasy), ketamine (Special K), and gamma hydroxybutyrate (GHB), along with performance-enhancing drugs such as sildenafil during marathon drug and sex parties. Such parties take place in public bathhouses or are arranged at private apartments via websites and internet chat rooms. "Circuit parties"—initially organised around AIDS awareness—take participants from city to city and are increasingly becoming vehicles for new transmissions, Berger says.

"No matter what your boundaries are sober, there is no boundary on crystal—your inhibition completely dissolves", says Kevin Osten, who works with metamphetamine addicts as primary therapist for intensive outpatient care at Chicago Lakeshore Hospital, a psychiatric care provider.

A Rise in Unsafe Sexual Encounters

Keith, who frequently sought drug and sex partners on the internet, says that with metamphetamine encounters, the question of HIV status was rarely broached. "Unless you told me otherwise, I would assume you were positive", he said. "Safe-sex rules do not apply with crystal meth."

Eventually, Keith began having trouble remembering the names and faces of the dozens of men with whom he had had unprotected sex.

Health officials say another reason for the rise in unsafe sexual encounters is the common perception in the gay community that HIV is now manageable thanks to new treatment drugs. Once addicted to metamphetamines, however, users on treatment begin to find it difficult to comply with the HIV treatment's strict dosage regimen.

In addition, many metamphetamine users inject the drug, increasing their risk of contracting HIV and other blood borne diseases like hepatitis. "What we're seeing in New York, Chicago, and Atlanta is a replica of what we saw in San Francisco", says Alex Kral, director of Urban Health Studies at the University of California, San Francisco. "I wouldn't be surprised if we see an upsurge in HIV and hepatitis C in those areas", he says.

Kral says that in the San Francisco area, 90% of injection users have hepatitis C, and nationally, that number ranges from 50–90%.

But some experts are sceptical that increased HIV infection rates can be directly attributed to the spread of metamphetamine use alone. A more important factor may be the common perception among many in the gay community that HIV infection is now less of a threat because of the success of new treatments. Michael Clatts, director of New York's Institute for International Research on Youth at Risk, believes that an effective response to the current HIV crisis must focus on unsafe sex practices not just drugs. Many men who are putting themselves at risk, he says, are not regular metamphetamine users.

"It's too simplistic to solely link drugs and sexual risk. It's going to require a complex public response. It's not going to be credible to guys who use speed, many of them in a controlled way, to tell them the sky's falling", Clatts says.

Improving Public Health Programs

Experts do agree that so far public health officials have been unprepared for the risk posed by the upsurge of metamphetamine use in the gay community. Most HIV-prevention programmes have developed one set of messages for the gay community and another set for drug users.

"Gay populations aren't being reached by the same messages or prevention programmes as other injection drug users", said Kral. Most federal dollars, he says, have been spent on research on pharmacological treatments of metamphetamine addiction—so far without success—instead of on more holistic behavioural, cultural, and epidemiological approaches.

Steve Shoptaw, a research psychologist at the Integrated Substance Abuse Programs at University of California, Los Angeles, says he and his colleagues have been developing programmes specifically for gay men who are using metamphetamine. "It's important, because by the time gay men show up at the clinic door, three out of five are HIV positive", he says.

In a recent study, Shoptaw and his co-workers combined cognitive behavioural training tailored to men who have sex with men with a contingency management programme that rewarded participants for staying off drugs. Drug urine tests were done three times a week. Participants who remained clean were rewarded with a graduated voucher system, which allowed them to earn up to US$1200 for vouchers to cover activities and purchases that would help maintain a clean lifestyle, such as travel to visit family members or transport to work.

The combined treatment approach showed a three-fold reduction in the number of days of metamphetamine use and a three-fold reduction in the frequency of unprotected sex in the days before clinic visits. What is unique about the study, says Shoptaw, is that a treatment programme targeting drug use is also showing improvement at reducing sexual risk.

A national conference will be held on the problem later [in 2005.] The conference, Methamphetamines, HIV and Hepatitis, is being organised by the Harm Reduction Project, a non-profit group based in Salt Lake City, Utah, dedicated to reaching out to marginalised groups to reduce the social and physical harm caused by risk-taking behaviours such as drug use.

According to Harm Reduction Project executive director Luciano Colonna, the conference will bring health workers and researchers from the public and private sectors together with law enforcement officials to discuss strategies to combat the rise in metamphetamine use in both heterosexual and gay, as well as rural and urban communities. "We would like to see education, prevention, treatment, and response, with science being the guiding light versus judgment or quick fixes", he said.

6

Condoms Prevent the Spread of AIDS

M. Monica Sweeney and Rita Kirwan Grisman

M. Monica Sweeney is an assistant clinical professor of preventive medicine at the State University of New York (SUNY) Health Science Center of Brooklyn. Rita Kirwan Grisman is a commercial writer.

The only way to protect oneself from HIV transmission caused by sexual intercourse is by using latex condoms correctly and consistently 100 percent of the time. Condoms undergo rigorous testing to ensure that the virus that causes AIDS cannot penetrate them. People throughout the world, especially in Africa and India, must be educated about safe sex and have condoms made available. Unless condom use increases, millions of people will continue to die.

Without condom protection you are vulnerable to HIV transmission from vaginal, anal, or oral sex. According to the *Journal of Sexually Transmitted Diseases*, the risks of HIV transmission are 10,000 times greater among non-condom users than among the population that uses condoms all the time. Stated more optimistically, condom use during intercourse is 10,000 times safer than not using a condom.

The good news is this: used consistently and correctly, latex condoms are 98 percent effective. Therefore, to provide maximum protection, condoms must be used *consistently*, 100 percent of the time, and they must be used *correctly* 100 percent of the time. Unfortunately, 100 percent condom use is so unusual that the very idea of it is, for all intents and purposes, theoretical. However, one of my patients in her mid-thirties says she doesn't know what it feels like to have sex without a condom, since she never has. It can be done!—and must be done, because using condoms can save your life.

How Condoms Protect Against AIDS

How do condoms prevent transmission of the AIDS virus? Simple: the virus that causes AIDS cannot penetrate latex. The virus is too large to escape latex pores. Condoms are double-dipped in latex, and the manufacturing process is so rigorous as to seem almost fanatical. The language on the packages— "triple tested," "individually electronically tested," "maximum reliability"—may sound like hype, but it's not. Different companies may use different methods to arrive at the efficacy of their products, and may advertise it using different terms. But whatever the language or methods, they all have identical standards to measure up to, standards set by that very tough taskmaster, the Food and Drug Administration (FDA). Those standards apply to all condoms sold in the United States, whether they are manufactured here or not.

Every condom approved by the FDA must pass an electric pinhole test, in which the condom is fitted onto a metal form called a mandrel in an intense electrical field. Rubber doesn't conduct electricity, so no electricity reaches the metal from under the condom unless the condom has a pinhole in it, in which case an indicator light goes off and the condom is rejected. The entire manufacturing lot in which that condom was found is tossed.

That's just one test.

There's a tensile test where equipment measures the condom's strength. The dimensions test precisely measures the length, width and thickness of a batch of condoms. When more than four out of 100 tested don't conform to an acceptable range, that entire lot from which the samples were taken is destroyed. There's an air burst properties test, a leakage test and a package integrity test, during which condom wrappers are checked for wrapper leaks.

Teaching People About Condoms

Need more evidence that condoms are effective? Consider this: do you think Bill Gates would pour $200 million into a project that he didn't believe would work?

In December 2003, in Mysore, India, Bill and Melinda Gates began a program to provide information and condoms to those most at risk for contracting AIDS and passing it on—sex workers, soldiers, migrant workers, and truck drivers. The information and condoms are distributed at clinics set up especially for the population at greatest risk. In sessions at these clinics, referred to as "Tea and Condoms," the audience is taught about safe sex, behavior modification, and HIV; and condoms are distributed. Health workers roam the streets to preach their condom/safe sex message, as well as to round up likely students for more comprehensive sessions at the clinics.

Individuals must act responsibly to stop [AIDS].

Just assembling citizenry to educate is not always easy, for India as a nation is shy about sex. The nation that produced the Kama Sutra, which emboldened many a generation to try stuff it never learned in sex education classes, doesn't want to discuss its famous export with health workers. Nonetheless, many anxious Indians are gratefully participating in long-overdue conversations about sex and reluctantly accepting gifts of condoms. The project is still too new to have yielded statistics, but there's no shortage of evidence for the effectiveness of condoms.

For example, in 1986 in Uganda, the devastating AIDS epidemic started to slow when the country developed a national campaign to accomplish a fundamental change in the nation's sexual behavior. The campaign was so simple, it seems almost impossible to believe that it worked. Referred to as the ABC, this is what it was: A. Abstain, and delay the age at which sexual activity commences. B. Be faithful. C. Use condoms if A and B fail. The president of Uganda often added D: if you don't do ABC you will die. The success of the program in Uganda (a decrease in new HIV cases from 20 percent a year to 6 percent from 1992 to 2000) can be largely attributed to the country's president, who believed in it and put resources behind it. . . .

The Best Protection

A 1993 U.S. study published in the *Journal of Acquired Immune Deficiency Syndromes* found that among 171 uninfected women having sex with HIV-infected partners (called discordant couples) who used condoms, only two contracted the virus. That's about 1.2 percent. In another study about the same time, eight out of ten women whose partners didn't use condoms every time became infected. That's *80 percent.*

It's no secret that *condoms are the best protection against the transmission of the Human Immunodeficiency Virus that technology currently offers.* Yet 87 percent of discordant couples do not use condoms consistently. Is it any wonder people are dying by the millions?

Individuals must act responsibly to stop this disease. However, responsible action requires information and access to options. In some places—maybe closer than you think—information and options are being blocked, and people are dying.

7

Condoms Do Not Prevent the Spread of Sexually Transmitted Diseases

Steve Cable

Steve Cable is a research associate with Probe Ministries, a non-profit ministry whose goal is to spread the Christian faith throughout the world.

Condom use does not protect people from sexually transmitted diseases, in particular the human papillomavirus (HPV), a disease that can cause cervical cancer. College women have a 38 percent chance of contracting the virus within a year of becoming sexually active, even if their male partners always use a condom. Therefore, media claims that condom use reduces the risk of becoming infected are not only false but also dangerous. The only ways to avoid STDs are abstinence or a monogamous relationship.

If terrorists were caught attempting to manipulate the environment at America's colleges and universities so that 85 percent of all coeds would graduate infected with a life threatening virus, they would be vilified and prosecuted to the full extent of the law. Many media reports on a recent study about the effectiveness of condom use in deterring the spread of HPV [human papillomavirus] have the potential to produce the same result. Irresponsible and/or ignorant journalism producing a false sense of security may be able to accomplish what the most sophisticated terrorist operation would be unable to pull off.

Steve Cable, "Despite Media Claims, Condoms Don't Prevent STDs," www.probe.org, 2006. Reproduced by permission.

Studies Show That Condoms Are Ineffective

Human papilloma virus (HPV)—which can cause cervical cancer, genital warts and vaginal, vulvar, anal and penile cancers—is the most common sexually transmitted disease, infecting about 80 percent of young women within five years of becoming sexually active. One of the arguments for abstinence prior to marriage is that condoms have not been shown to be effective in protecting against HPV and other sexually transmitted diseases. A new study report, published in the June 22nd (2006) edition of the *New England Journal of Medicine*, is entitled "Condom Use and the Risk of Genital Human Papillomavirus Infection in Young Women." This study was structured to provide better information on the impact of male condom use on the likelihood of women contracting HPV.

Any woman who is sexually active with multiple partners during their college years will almost certainly contract HPV.

What new insights are gained from this study on the relationship of condom use and HPV? The most important result is that sexually active college women whose male partners used condoms 100 percent of the time (both with the woman in the study and with other sexual partners) have roughly a 38 percent chance of contracting HPV within the first year of becoming sexually active. If she has at least one different partner per year for four years, the probability that she will leave college with an HPV infection is greater than 85 percent. The obvious conclusion of the study is that condom use is not an effective means of preventing HPV.

The study did find that sexually active college women whose male partners used condoms less than 100 percent of the time had a probability of contracting HPV within the first year of becoming sexually active ranging from 62 percent to virtually 100 percent depending upon the regularity of condom use by their male partners. Although the study does show that male condom use did reduce the probability of sexually active women contracting HPV, it did not reduce it to a level that any thinking person would consider safe. Based on the study results, it is reasonable to conclude that any woman who is sexually active with multiple partners during their college years will almost certainly contract HPV whether they ensure their partners use condoms or not.

One would expect the headlines for the media reports on this topic to read, "Condoms Shown to Be Ineffective Against HPV." The body of the article would point out that these results vindicate the proponents of abstinence emphasis in preventing the spread of sexually transmitted diseases. However, the exact opposite is being purported by the media. Here are some samples from the headlines:

- Condoms Reduce HPV Risk After All, Without Increasing Likelihood of Sex (American Council on Science and Health)

- Condoms Proven to Protect Against Virus (Associated Press, *Yuma Sun*)

- Condoms Reduce Risk of Cervical Cancer, Survey Says (*Dallas Morning News*, June 22, 2006)

A Dangerous Half-Truth

These headlines take a half truth and present it in a way that is designed to further a political agenda while endangering the health of America's youth and young adults. Even more dangerous is the first line of the Associated Press report, "For the first time, scientists have proof that condoms offer women impressive protection against the virus that causes cervical cancer." I do not consider an 85 percent chance of catching the virus in four years "impressive." I would consider it dismal! The AP report then adds insult to injury by including this quote from an obscure expert:

That's pretty awesome. There aren't too many times when you can have an intervention that would offer so much protection, said Dr. Patricia Kloser, an infectious-disease specialist at the University of Medicine and Dentistry of New Jersey who was not a part of the study.

The use of the words "impressive protection" and "so much protection" in conjunction with the results of this study borders on criminal. We need to hold our journalists to task for such biased (or, in the best case, shoddy) reporting. Even more important, we need to get out the real conclusion supported by the study: Abstinence or a completely monogamous relationship is the only effective protection against sexually transmitted diseases. As Christians, we would point to marriage as the only valid venue for a monogamous relationship, but that is outside the scope of the study.

Reduce Sexual Activity, Reduce the Spread of HPV

To determine the number of coeds at risk, we need to consider how many are sexually active. In order to participate in this study, the college coeds had to have refrained from vaginal intercourse prior to the two weeks preceding the start of the study. In other words, the participants were virgins at the beginning of the study. Over the three year study period, 45 percent of those originally enrolled remained virgins. According to a report from the U.S. Center for Disease Control, in 2002, 70 percent of never married teens under the age of 18 had not engaged in sex. Taking the 55 percent from the study who started sexual activity in college with the 30 percent who were already sexually active, one would predict that 68.5 percent of college coeds would be sexually active. This tracks well with the CDC data that 68 percent of never married females have engaged in sex before they were 20. Thus, if coed sexual activity remains at the same level and 100 percent condom use is practiced, we can expect approximately 60 percent of college coeds to graduate with an HPV versus 68 percent with 50 percent condom usage. In contrast, if we could cut the number of sexually active coeds in half, the HPV infection rate among graduates could drop to 33 percent or less regardless of condom usage.

America's Plan to Fight AIDS in Africa Is Hypocritical

Sanjay Basu

Sanjay Basu is a doctor who has written frequently on AIDS and HIV for publications such as Nature *and* Science.

President Bush's plan to fight the global AIDS crisis is destructive and hypocritical. Although the White House claims to support the Global Fund for AIDS, TB, and Malaria, its AIDS policy is mainly geared toward funding USAIDS, which is focused on abstinence-based prevention and not on providing comprehensive care to people with AIDS or HIV. White House policy also undercuts the ability of AIDS victims in developing countries from receiving generic drugs that could improve and extend their lives. The consequences of these destructive policies are poverty and job loss, economic problems that lead to prostitution and an increase in transmission of the virus.

Winning praise from the editorial staffs of the *Washington Post* and the *New York Times*, [President George W.] Bush's AIDS plan has been described as a wonderful "surprise" to those working against the global pandemic—a turnaround from previous policy, especially for a White House that has for so long been strongly connected to the patent-based pharmaceutical industry. Even some major NGOs [nongovernmental organizations] sat back in awe at the prospect

Sanjay Basu, "Behind Dramatic Declarations: Bush's AIDS Plan," ZNet.org, February 4, 2003. Reproduced by permission of the author.

of a $15 billion contribution to AIDS (including $10 billion in new monies) from the Bush White House. The plan is to include treatment—not just prevention—with generic medicines.

But behind the rhetoric of the State of the Union lay a much darker picture of White House policy. In the fine print of the Bush AIDS proposal is a constant with previous policies: the plan, first of all, excludes 36 of the highest burden African countries from receiving funds. The $15 billion is also spread over five years (making it about equivalent to the rounding error on the defense budget), and nearly all but $200 million a year will be routed through mechanisms other than the Global Fund for AIDS, TB and Malaria. The Global Fund contribution, in other words, is unchanged. This reflects a continuation of White House policy to undercut the Global Fund (preventing future, multilateral commitments) while claiming to support anti-AIDS efforts. Previous AIDS funds have also been consistently directed to USAID instead of the Global Fund—and USAID's programs (which almost totally exclude treatment, except for four pilot projects) have become notorious for failing to provide appropriate, comprehensive care, as well as for "lapsing" into abstinence-based-prevention-mode. The funds seem to be magically "redistributed" away to other programs periodically. The Global Fund, meanwhile, has declared bankruptcy as of last Friday [January 31, 2003].

Undercutting Generic Drugs

But an even darker part of this AIDS plan relates to its policy on generic drugs. Bush declared that AIDS drug prices have lowered to $300 per year—which is correct, if you are purchasing from generic manufacturers. The problem is that the US Trade Representative (USTR) has threatened poor countries around the world with trade sanctions (using what it calls the Special 301 Watch List), forcing them to change their intellectual property rules to be more stringent than those required by the World Trade Organization. Two of the main types of antiretroviral drugs—nevirapine and 3TC—will be illegal to import to 37 of the African countries covered by the Bush proposal precisely because of the consistent pressure of the USTR to prevent generic competition for the U.S. pharmaceutical industry. While the Bush plan claims to support generic funding, the policies of the USTR under Bush simultaneously undercut the possibility of actual generic use.

The story doesn't end there. [In December 2002,] at a WTO council meeting, trade ministers from around the world were to settle on the mechanism by which poor countries without the capacity to produce medicines were to import cheap generic drugs. In November of 2001, at the Doha conference of the WTO, the USTR and other trade ministers signed a declaration to allow "access to medicines for all" on the premise that intellectual property should be secondary to public health. They decided to also agree to a mechanism (by December 2002) that would determine how generics could be produced for exportation to poor countries without manufacturing capacity. Such a declaration sounds charitable, but the fact that it had to be declared is bordering on perverse. No one bothered to mention that a vast amount of the research and development on AIDS drugs (sometimes through the clinical trial stage) was paid for through tax payer funds directed through the National Institutes of Health (NIH) to divisions of the NIH and to universities: d4T was researched under the National Cancer Institute and Yale, ddl under the NIH, 3TC under Emory and Yale, nevirapine under NIAID and the NIH, and AZT under the NIH and the National Cancer Institute. Similar R&D histories exist for nearly all classes of medicines.

But in spite of these facts, the December 2002 meeting turned into a stalemate. Rather than decide on a clear mechanism to allow generics to be produced for exportation to the poorest of countries, the USTR decided to "reinterpret" the declaration made at the Doha conference, claiming that it applied only to a limited number of diseases, and also claiming that the countries most able to produce medicines could not export to poor countries. Even the legal mechanism for allowing exportation was to be woefully complex, effectively rendering generic competition impossible. The talks broke down after the USTR refused to negotiate. Even the EU trade minister blamed the USTR's stubbornness for the lack of access to medicines, calling it representative of the pharmaceutical industry's "stupid" position.

The industry, and the USTR, claims that generics would undermine the capacity to pay for research and development—that is, the research and development that American taxpayers actually foot most of the bill for. The industry doesn't bother to release its own tax information, however, which reveals that Merck [in 2002] used 13% of its profits on marketing and only 5% on R&D, Pfizer spent 35% on marketing and only 15% on R&D, and the industry overall spent 27% on marketing and 11% on R&D according to the Securities and Exchange Commission. That's not accounting for the fact that 52% of new drugs on the market aren't even the result of R&D, but are "me too" drugs that are simple reformulations of old products slapped with new stickers.

The industry still claims that generics will undermine its business, even as it continues to be ranked by Fortune Magazine as the world's most profitable industry for 11 years in a row (having profits as a percentage of revenue nearly three times the rest of the Fortune 500 industry). When confronted with the fact that Africa comprises only 1.3% of the industry's revenues (making its loss equivalent to "about three days fluctuation in exchange rates," according to an industry analyst quoted in the *Washington Post*), the industry claims that generic drugs will get diverted to the North to undermine its key markets, and cites GlaxoSmithKline's recent loss of AIDS drugs sent to Africa as a case in point. But a look at the GSK case shows that Glaxo failed to even track the shipments and only discovered after a year that its packages to Africa had been shipped improperly, allowing them to be smuggled to Europe. Tracking mechanisms, however, seem to be no trouble for neighborhood flower shops. Indian generic manufacturers, meanwhile, have shipped medicines for over two decades without a single case of "diversion".

The economic and social effects of the free trade agreements are precisely those that spread AIDS.

But based on the rhetoric—and the $20 million in campaign contributions (hard and soft)—of the patent-based pharmaceutical industry, the USTR and the White House have decided to continue their campaign against generic drugs. While losing the support of even the EU at the WTO, the USTR has decided that if it can't multilaterally cut off access to cheaper medicines for the poor, it will do so through bilateral and regional trade agreements. So the current draft of the Free Trade Area of the Americas excludes key public health protections and creates mechanisms far too difficult to achieve generic access. One common mechanism used by the USTR is to force one country to have another country pass legislation for exportation of goods. In other words, India's government would have to pass legislation to authorize exportation of medicines from Indian companies to Pakistanis. What a politically feasible plan! The USTR is expanding such a model in a second agreement with a group of Latin American countries, a plan for sub-Saharan countries, and for bilateral deals with countries like Morocco and Jordan.

Poverty Leads to AIDS

Cutting off medicine access isn't the only hypocritical part of the Bush AIDS plan, however. The deeper problem is not just one of medicine access—it's that the economic and social effects of the free trade agreements are precisely those that spread AIDS. Epidemiologists and physicians have agreed that the number one epidemiological correlate to AIDS (and TB, and a number of other infectious and non-infectious diseases) is poverty. We saw the nasty effects of NAFTA on the health of Mexicans, and now the Free Trade Area of the Americas' (FTAA) deal will expand that to the entire Western hemisphere. Migration in Thailand, as Walden Bello has shown, resulted from IMF packages there that destroyed rural agricultural systems and broke up families as laborers traveled to Bangkok for work. Marriages split, women lost jobs and entered into prostitution for work, and AIDS and TB spread among the poorest. The same trends have been established elsewhere. The excessive focus on "individual behavior" in public discourse on AIDS neglects the fact that most people in the world—according to broad surveys—know how HIV is transmitted. People scratch their heads at the continual prevalence of "risk behaviors" in spite of this, but it's not so surprising. If there's no food on the table, and prostitution is the only work available, doesn't prostitution make sense? If Anglo America destroys agricultural systems to set up a mine, and laborers from hundreds of miles away travel there for pittance, spending six-to-seven days a week in all-male barracks, what happens when the company decides to "keep the workers happy" by supplying them with alcohol and prostitutes on breaks? The issue is not so much "behavior" as much as the conditions under which such behavior occurs.

And so the Bush AIDS plan may seem miraculous, and indeed it does add some funds to AIDS programs. But AIDS has become increasingly commodified, treated as a problem that can be solved with declarations while the broader public health and socioeconomic context in which it occurs is ignored. And that is the real problem with the Bush AIDS plan: as one hand provides a poor, leaky bandage, the other cuts deeper into the wound.

9

Young People Must Be Educated About AIDS

Steve Berry

Steve Berry is a writer for Avert, an international HIV and AIDS charity.

The only way to fight the AIDS epidemic is by educating young people. Young adults need to know that unprotected sex places them at high risk for becoming infected. They also need to know that sexual abstinence until marriage will protect them from infection, as will always using a condom when engaging in intercourse. However, these lessons must not be accompanied by moral judgments or abstinence-only education, because those approaches misinform adolescents and can make them feel stigmatized if they are sexually active. Schools, the media, and peers should participate in AIDS education in order to ensure that all young people are reached.

The HIV epidemic has been spreading steadily for the past two decades, and now affects every country in the world. Each year, more people die and the number of people living with HIV continues to rise—in spite of the fact that we have developed many proven HIV prevention methods. We now know much more about how HIV is transmitted than we did in the early days of the epidemic, and we know much more about how we can prevent it being transmitted. One of the key means of HIV prevention is education—teaching people about HIV: what it is, what it does, and how people can protect themselves. Over half of the world's population is now under 25 years old. This age group is more threatened by AIDS than any other; equally it is the group that has more power to fight the epidemic than any other. Education can help to fight HIV, and it must focus on young people.

There are two main reasons that AIDS education for young people is important:

- To prevent them from becoming infected.

  Young people are often particularly vulnerable to sexually-transmitted HIV, and to HIV infection as a result of drug-use. Young people (5–24 years old) account for half of all new HIV infections worldwide— more than 6,000 become infected with HIV every day. More than a third of all people living with HIV or AIDS are under the age of 25, and almost two-thirds of them are women. In many parts of the world, young people in this age-group are at particularly high risk of HIV infection from unprotected sex, sex between men and IV drug-use because of the very high prevalence rates often found amongst people who engage in these behaviours. Young people are also often especially vulnerable to exploitation that may increase their susceptibility to infection. Even if they are not currently engaging in risk behaviours, as they become older, young people may soon be exposed to situations that put them at risk. Indeed, globally, most young people become sexually active in their teens. The fact that they are—or soon will be—at risk of HIV infection makes young people a crucial target for AIDS education.

- To reduce stigma and discrimination.

  People who are infected with HIV around the world often suffer terribly from stigma, in that people who are HIV+ are somehow thought to be 'dirty', or to have 'brought it on themselves' by 'immoral practises'.

They often experience discrimination in terms of housing, medical care, and employment. These experiences, aside from being extremely distressing for HIV+ people, can also have the effect of making people reluctant to be tested for HIV, in case they are found to be HIV+. Stigma and discrimination often starts early—as name-calling amongst children. AIDS education can help to prevent this, halting stigma and discrimination before they have an opportunity to grow.

AIDS Is Treated As a Moral Issue

The problem seems to stem from the fact that HIV is often sexually transmitted, or is transmitted via drug use. Any subject that concerns sex between young people or drug use tends to be seen from a moralistic perspective—many adults, particularly those of the religious right—believe that teens need to be prevented from indulging in these high-risk activities. They believe that young people shouldn't—and don't need to be—provided with any education about these subjects, other than to be told that they are 'wrong', and not to do such things. Unfortunately, however, adults have been trying to stop young people from having sex and taking drugs for many, many years with little success, so this method alone seems unlikely to offer any real relief in the AIDS epidemic.

There are other difficulties in taking an exclusively moral approach to HIV education. Firstly, this is what tends to perpetuate stigmatisation of HIV+ people. By teaching young people that indulging in 'immoral' sex and drugs will lead to HIV infection, educators imply that anyone who is HIV+ is therefore involved in these 'immoral' activities. This stigmatisation tends to make people reluctant to be tested for HIV, and therefore more inclined to remain ignorant of their status—and perhaps go on to infect others. AIDS education shouldn't ever include a moral judgement—it is one thing to teach young people that promiscuous sex and intravenous drug use are unsafe, another thing to teach them that these things are *morally wrong*.

Many AIDS educators around the world are disturbed at this growing trend to provide AIDS education from a moralistic perspective, and argue that AIDS education ought to be non-judgemental, teaching what the dangers are and how they can be avoided—without passing moral judgement on those who engage in infection-related behaviours, whether they do so safely or not.

The opposing, more conservative viewpoint, however, argues that young people shouldn't be taught about sexual health and drug-related dangers at all. They feel that teaching them about these things, even teaching about their dangers, may encourage young people to indulge in these risk behaviours. Research suggests that this is not the case at all, and certainly young people themselves tend to be very definite about the fact that they need sex and sexual health education. Unfortunately, curriculum planners tend not to listen to the young people who will be their students. This viewpoint can result in no AIDS education at all being offered.

> *"I did not go to school and learn about the civil war and decide to start a civil war, nor would I have had sex because of a class in school."*—Mark

However, many young people become sexually active long before adults would prefer them to do so, or expect them to do, and teens are not all 'innocent'. Quite simply, if teens are having sex, they need sexual health information. Fortunately, many curriculum planners and legislators have recognised this, and provide young people in many countries with abstinence-plus or comprehensive sex [and] HIV education. . . .

Different Approaches to AIDS Education for Young People

Most countries in the world offer teens some sort of sexual health and HIV education in their schools at some stage. AIDS education can also be targeted at young people in nonschool environments—through their peers, through the media, and through doctors or their parents. In some countries, individual schools are allowed to determine what AIDS education they will offer. In other countries, this is determined by legislation passed by central government. And in other countries—especially poor ones that are severely affected by HIV—AIDS education is imported by foreign governments, charities and NGOs [nongovernmental organizations] come in to the country and deliver AIDS education as part of a larger package of HIV prevention work.

Over 80% of abstinence-only curricula contained false or misleading information.

AIDS education for young people today falls generally into one of two categories—either abstinence-only or comprehensive. These are actually types of sex education, rather than AIDS education specifically—AIDS education in many schools comes as a part of a sex education program, if it occurs at all. The type of AIDS education program that is offered usually depends on the attitudes of those who determine the syllabus content—right wing organisations, many Christian organisations, and the family-values lobby tend to prefer abstinence-only education, while those who feel that preventing young people from becoming infected with HIV is more important than keeping them ignorant about sexual behaviour—prefer comprehensive AIDS education.

Abstinence-only education teaches students that they must say no to sexual activity until they are married. This approach does not teach students anything about how to protect themselves from STDs or HIV, how pregnancy occurs or how to prevent it, and teaches about homosexuality and masturbation only as far as to say that they are wrong. Those who favour this method of education claim that teaching young people about sex will make them want to try it—thus increasing their risk of contracting HIV, amongst other things.

Abstinence-only education is popular in America, especially so now that it has a Republican President. A House of Representatives report at the end of 2004 found that over 80% of abstinence-only curricula contained false or misleading information—something that is worrying now not only for those in America but increasingly for the rest of the world, as America exports its HIV-prevention and education attitudes to parts of the world with a much higher HIV prevalence. This is particularly worrying in that abstinence-only programmes have been shown not only to fail to reduce the numbers of STD infections and unplanned pregnancies seen in pupils, but recent studies indicate that they might actually be related to an increase in these problems.

Comprehensive AIDS education teaches about sexual abstinence until marriage, and teaches that it is one way of protecting yourself from HIV transmission, STDs and unwanted pregnancy. It also teaches that there are other ways of preventing these things, such as condom use. People who favour this approach take the perspective that young people should be taught to remain sexually abstinent until marriage, but that there will always be some who won't—and that they must be provided with the information to enable them to protect themselves. This type of education also teaches not only about the dangers of drug use, but also about methods of HIV-prevention that drug users can employ—the use of clean needles, for example.

Abstinence-Plus Education

Abstinence-only and comprehensive AIDS education have been combined to produce abstinence-plus education. This type of education focuses on sexual abstinence until marriage as the preferred method of protection, but also provides information about contraception, sexuality and disease prevention.

Many abstinence-only campaigners complain that abstinence-plus and comprehensive education are the same thing, although abstinence-plus educators claim that this type of course contains more focus on sexual abstinence until marriage.

There has been debate for many years over which form of sex education is most effective in terms of preventing underage sex, unwanted pregnancy and STD and HIV transmission—although most studies seem to show that comprehensive sex and AIDS education is at least as effective as abstinence-only—and probably more so. However, currently the trend in America—and which is being exported to much of the developing world—is towards abstinence-only education. If it is as unsuccessful as studies indicate it to be, then we can expect this morality-induced type of education become responsible for an increase in HIV figures amongst the young, especially in high-prevalence parts of the world to which America has taken its methods.

Fifteen percent of Americans believe that schools should teach only about abstinence from sexual intercourse and should not provide information on how to obtain and use condoms and other contraception. Forty-six percent believe that the most appropriate approach is abstinence-plus. Almost half of those surveyed felt that the word 'abstinence' included not only sexual intercourse, but 'passionate kissing' and 'masturbation', too.

AIDS Education Outside the Classroom

Not all young people are fortunate enough to attend school. This might be for one of a variety of reasons—in some countries, it is necessary to pay for schooling. Poor families may be unable to afford to send a child to school, or may be unable to send all their children to school. Sometimes children will be required to work, making them unavailable for school. In other areas, young people may live in areas where a local school is not accessible. In some situations, young people may have been excluded from school for reasons that might be due to the young person's behaviour, academic or intellectual abilities, or due to discrimination. Some young people play truant, and will have only very limited attendance. The proportion of young people who attend school differs markedly in various parts of the world.

Clearly, although AIDS education offered through the school might reach many young people, it will not reach all, and other forms of education are required.

One of these is the media. Most young people will, at some time, be exposed to the media—this can include newspapers, television, books, radio—and also traditional media such as street performances or murals. One advantage of media-based AIDS education is that it can target specific groups amongst the population—if the message is to be targeted at young people, then it will be placed in media that are favoured by this audience. Many countries have tried some form of AIDS education advertisements, films, or announcements—a good example of this is the *LoveLife* campaign in South Africa—an education program 'by young people, for young people'. *LoveLife* used eye-catching posters and billboards to tell young people that sex was fun—but that it could be dangerous, too. The campaign also inserted its message into TV soaps that were popular with young people, and used rap and *kwaito* music to get its message across.

Prevention is the only way in which we can place any limits on the [AIDS] epidemic.

There are problems with media-based campaigns, too, however—it is hard to know to what extent the AIDS information has reached young people, and it is difficult to gain continued funding for initiatives whose success is so hard to measure.

Another way in which young people receive information about sex and HIV is through their peers. This is something that happens anyway to a great extent—many young people receive their first information about sexuality from their friends, although this information is often distorted and inaccurate. This type of peer education can be harnessed, though, and used to convey accurate, targeted information. Peer education is, quite simply, the process by which a group is given information by one of their peers who has received training and accurate information. This is a method often used with groups which have been marginalised, and might have cause to distrust information given to them by an authority figure—whereas they will listen to someone who is identifiably a member of their own group. This method of information-provision is often used with such groups as sex workers, the homeless, or drug-users. There is no reason that this method shouldn't be used with young people, however—and in many parts of the world, it *is* used. Indeed, it is particularly appropriate for young people who do not attend schools and will not have an opportunity to benefit from an AIDS education curriculum.

AIDS Education for the Future

Although the debate continues about how much—if any—AIDS education young people should receive, studies continue to show that being informed about the facts and the dangers of HIV and AIDS enables young people to protect themselves and is a crucial tool in the battle against HIV. There is no cure or vaccine for HIV—prevention is the only way in which we can place any limits on the epidemic. One of the most economical and effective means of HIV prevention is education—involving young people themselves in the HIV prevention effort.

On a global level, America's disposition towards the promotion of abstinence-only education is cause for concern. America's spending on HIV prevention around the world exceeds that of any other country, and is to be welcomed—as long as it doesn't use this money to promote its pro-abstinence-only views of AIDS education. These views—which have been shown to be less successful than comprehensive AIDS education techniques which *include* an abstinence element—may prove to be damaging to America's domestic AIDS prevention work. When exported to high-prevalence countries in Africa, they could prove disastrous.

Whenever educators and planners ask, and listen to young people, they are told time and time again that young people overwhelmingly ask for adequate AIDS education. In most parts of the world, this means *more* AIDS education than they are presently getting. Young people know that they have the right to the information that enables them to safeguard their lives and those of their sexual partners—they must be listened to, and provided with that information clearly, openly and honestly.

10

Abstinence-Only Education Is Effective

Janice Shaw Crouse

Janice Shaw Crouse is a senior fellow at the Concerned Women for America's Beverly LaHaye Institute.

Schools must teach teenagers that the only way to avoid sexually transmitted diseases is by remaining abstinent until marriage. Despite the claims made by sexual education programs, condoms are unreliable and do not protect people from STDs. Fifteen million young adults are infected with STDs every year, a statistic that could fall sharply if abstinence-only education becomes more common. The leftist ideology that opposes abstinence education needs to realize that sexual activity destroys the lives of teenagers.

In Rhode Island, Education Commissioner Peter McWalters issued a directive forbidding schools in the state to use abstinence programs or materials. The official ban declares that abstinence programs violate student rights, contain sexist stereotypes and marginalize homosexual teens.

In a supportive statement, the president of Advocates for Youth, James Wagoner, claims that abstinence programs are "bad science" as well as "bad policy." Further, Wagoner declared that abstinence programs operate without "oversight" and that they are a "blatant violation of medical ethics and basic human rights." Unbelievably, Wagoner accused the abstinence initiatives of censoring and taking a position: "stay pure

Janice Shaw Crouse, "Abstinence Education Banned," cwfa.org, March 28, 2006. Reproduced by permission.

or we don't care about you." Calling federal funding for abstinence programs a "national scandal," Wagoner asked Congress for an immediate moratorium on spending for the programs.

Supposedly, Mr. Wagoner and Commissioner McWalters are open-minded people who support diversity in education and want teens to have as much information as possible before making pivotal decisions that affect their lives and future. Yes, right!

Sexual Activity Harms Teenagers

With such passionate, knee-jerk reactions, one has to wonder what motivates these two men and where they have been over the past 20 years (they are education experts, after all) when the results of teen sexual activity have so negatively affected teens' futures.

- Since they care so deeply about teenagers, could it be that they haven't noticed the results of teen sexual activity: high pregnancy rates, skyrocketing rates of sexually transmitted diseases (STDs), or the integral relationship between teen pregnancy and school drop-outs with subsequent poverty?

- Or maybe they have not seen the dramatic increases in teen depression, violence, suicides and risky behavior that have increased as teen sexual activity increases.

- Perhaps they haven't noticed that the long dominance of liberal programs produced increased sexual activity instead of curbing such emotional involvements and risky behavior.

- Perhaps they have never made the connection between poor grades, alcohol and drug abuse, school drop-outs and other negative results that frequently accompany sexual involvement during the high school years.

- Perhaps they are unaware that since abstinence programs were instituted, sexual activity among high school students has declined more than 10 percent. Would they want to go on record complaining about that decrease?

More likely, these two education experts have bought into the leftist myths—that sex education programs provide the motivation for "safe" sex for teens, while condoms (when teens are taught to use them properly) provide the actual protection. Never mind the data about inconsistent use of condoms—even by adults—not to even mention the unreliability of condoms and the lack of protection they provide against certain STDs. Perhaps they truly believe that teens will wait until they are "old enough" or are "really in love" before engaging in sex. Anyone who has been around teenagers knows that they think they are already old enough for anything and "puppy love" is, to them, as real as it gets!

A Life or Death Matter

I'd like to remind the two education experts that every year another 15 million young people are infected with STDs, *more than* one-third of all American babies are born out-of-wedlock and the percentage continues to rise every year, 45 million abortions are the legacy of so-called "free love," 20 percent of AIDS cases are among college-age young people, there are now more than 2 dozen *incurable* STDs and the fastest spreading one is HPV, which can cause cervical cancer that kills over 5,000 women a year. Do they realize that having three or more sexual partners in a lifetime increases the odds of cervical cancer by 15 times? Have they seen the data indicating that teen sexual activity and drug use are linked? Are they aware of the connection between alcohol and teen sexual activity?

Sexual activity in high school *can* be a life or death matter.

There is a *huge* disparity between the funding for abstinence education and the funding for comprehensive sex education (\$12 to \$1). It is fair to say that the abstinence funding is a "drop in the bucket" compared to the comprehensive sex education funding. Even so, there has been a significant drop in teen sexual activity since abstinence education has been encouraged, and 10 scientific studies have proved the validity of the programs. Further, 85 percent of parents believe in emphasizing abstinence.

Counselors tell us that sexually active girls are three times more likely to be depressed than their abstinent peers. Among the boys, sexually active ones are depressed twice as often. Sexually active teens are more likely to attempt suicide (girls 15 percent to 5 percent and boys 6 percent to 1 percent). But the most telling fact is that fully 63 percent of teens regret early sexual activity and wish that they had waited longer.

Liberal experts who want to ban abstinence programs ought to have to sit in a school counselor's office for several hours every week to watch brokenhearted teens stream through, to see the emotional and psychological devastation—lives shattered and hopes for the future crashed on the shoals of leftist ideology perpetuated by radical experts with nothing to lose and a lot of federal funding to gain!

11

Abstinence-Only Education Is a Failure

Susan Hunter

Susan Hunter is an independent consultant who has worked with world health organizations.

Abstinence-only education, instead of reducing the spread of sexually transmitted diseases, has made teenagers and young adults more vulnerable to STDs. Teenagers whose sexual education discussed only abstinence are not aware that condoms will protect them from many STDs. They are also are more likely to engage in oral and anal sex because they want to avoid pregnancy and are unaware that STDs can be spread through those types of intercourse. Teenagers need to learn how to protect themselves during sexual activity; otherwise the social and medical costs of sexually transmitted diseases will rise.

In the age of HIV/AIDS, abstinence-only education is not just a poorly conceived experiment in public policy, it is a disaster that is already having severe effects on teen health and safety. HIV infections are increasing fastest in 18- to 24-year-olds, and nearly 60 percent of these are sex-related. Since teens are not taught realistic information about how to protect themselves, the number of infections will continue to grow over the coming years unless we come to our senses and help our children learn how to protect themselves. The HIV rate for American teens is already five times that of German

Susan Hunter, *Aids in America*. Basingstoke, Hampshire: Palgrave Macmillan, 2006.

adolescents. We are now reaping what we sowed with this first generation of abstinence-only teens left ignorant by their school systems, and we are likely to reap what we've sown for many years to come.

Paige and Tom [two young adults referenced by Hunter throughout the book] are but two of the millions of American children who were taught when they are at their youngest and most vulnerable that condoms are not effective against HIV. In fact, condoms are the only sure protection against all STDs for people who have sex. The people teens trust teach them nothing at all about the dangers they face in sexual experimentation, so they learn what they can from TV, the Internet, the library, and/or their friends.

Suppressing the Truth About STDs

U.S. Planned Parenthood argues that the Christian Right has been central to promoting the policy of abstinence-only education. Their white paper on adolescent sexuality says that "one of the most misguided and destructive messages that endangers adolescent health and life during this age of AIDS emanates from a vocal minority bent on suppressing or willfully ignoring the truth about sexual activity among adolescents in America. Under the guise of protecting our youth, they declare, inaccurately, that premarital sex among adolescents is a relatively new and corrupt social phenomenon.

> *Thanks to abstinence-only education, a whole generation of U.S. teens is threatened with HIV infection.*

"They are not content to teach that society should tolerate no sexual activity among adolescents," Planned Parenthood continues. "They say that if *any* sexuality education is to be offered at all in public schools, the only acceptable curriculum is one that not only endorses abstinence only and the post-

poning of sexual activity until marriage but also actively with-holds information on how to prevent pregnancy and sexually transmitted infections."

Like so many other young people in the United States who are now becoming infected with HIV, Paige and Tom learned the hard way that sexually transmitted diseases play for keeps. Few realize that sexually transmitted diseases, including herpes, chlamydia, hepatitis, gonorrhea, trichomoniasis, and syphilis as well as HIV can be transmitted by oral and anal as well as vaginal intercourse, and that unprotected anal sex is especially dangerous.

New data from the National Center for Health Statistics shows that one in three boys and one in four girls in the United States have had oral sex by age 15, increasing to 70 percent by age 19 for both boys and girls. This should not surprise us, because the practice is very common in our culture. By age forty-four, 90 percent of men and 88 percent of women have given or received oral sex, a proportion that increased only slightly from when it was measured ten years earlier. Anal sex is being tried by more Americans, and whites are more likely to have had both experiences than either blacks or Hispanics.

A Threat to Teenagers

The proportion of teens and young adults experimenting with oral and anal sex appear to have increased over prior surveys, although researchers say that the evidence is hard to interpret. What may be surprising to adults is that teens are adopting both practices at a very early age as a way of avoiding pregnancy and that girls are just as likely to get as to give oral sex.

Thanks to abstinence-only education, a whole generation of U.S. teens is threatened with HIV infection. In fact, research shows that the situation of "abstinent" teens is even worse than those who make no claims about their "purity." A 2004 study of 12,000 teens by Yale and Columbia Universities found that adolescents who pledged to remain virgins until marriage are four times more likely to take chances with anal sex than those who do not and are also less likely to use condoms.

The threat to our children can be easily contained. Study after study has shown that comprehensive sexual education has a positive effect on slowing teens' entry into the world of sex and ensuring that they take care of themselves when they do. The National Survey of Family Growth, which interviewed 1,280 teen girls between fifteen and nineteen, found that adolescents using birth control were no more sexually active than nonusers and were more likely to use protection when they had sex.

Perhaps the saddest footnote in the outrageous history of abstinence education in the United States is that the teen pregnancy rates and teen sexual activity were going down during the 1990s, thanks to comprehensive sexual education. Both pregnancy and reported sexual activity rates, used by public health officials as proxy indicators for safe sex behavior because STD rates are so hard to measure, were declining because teens were using condoms and were beginning to delay the start of their sexual lives.

Abstinence-only education began to have its effects in the late 1990s, when Paige was still in high school. Thanks to the misinformation handed out by these campaigns, a large number of the many American teens and young adults who have sex rarely protected themselves from pregnancy or infection. "When I was growing up," Paige said, "I had no idea about HIV/AIDS. I was just doing the same things everybody else does. You don't hear about it in Montana, you don't think about it. It only happens in the big cities, it only happens to minorities and gay men. I had a lot of ignorance about it."

Many teen coming-of-age behaviors put them at risk of HIV infection. More than 5 million U.S. teens—23 percent in a 2002 survey—said they had unprotected sex because of alcohol or drug abuse, cross-over behavior that contributes to rapid HIV spread. By the age of twenty-one, one in every five teens has received treatment for an STD. The direct medical costs of STDs for fifteen- to twenty-four-year-olds was $6.5 billion in 2000 alone.

12

The HPV Vaccine Is Safe and Effective

Centers for Disease Control

The Centers for Disease Control (CDC) is one of the components of the Department of Health and Human Services. The goals of the CDC include conducting research on public health and preventing the spread of infectious diseases.

The human papillomavirus vaccine, developed in 2006, is a safe and effective medicine that will protect girls and women from cervical cancer and other diseases that are caused by HPV. The vaccine is important because half of all sexually active people get HPV at some point in their lives, and each year thirty-seven hundred women die from cervical cancer in the United States. However, the vaccine does not protect against all forms of HPV that cause cervical cancer, so women still need regular screenings and Pap tests and should remain abstinent or monogamous if they want to reduce the risk of becoming infected.

In June 2006, the Advisory Committee on Immunization Practices (ACIP) voted to recommend the first vaccine developed to prevent cervical cancer and other diseases in females caused by certain types of genital human papillomavirus (HPV). The vaccine, Gardasil®, protects against four HPV types, which together cause 70% of cervical cancers and 90% of genital warts.

Centers for Disease Control, "HPV Vaccine Questions & Answers," http://www.cdc.gov/netinfo.htm, August 2006. Information obtained from the Centers for Disease Control (www.cdc.gov).

The Food and Drug Administration (FDA) recently licensed this vaccine for use in girls/women, ages 9–26 years. The vaccine is given through a series of three shots over a six-month period.

Recommendations for the Vaccine

The HPV vaccine is recommended for 11–12 year-old girls, and can be given to girls as young as 9. The vaccine is also recommended for 13–26 year-old girls/women who have not yet received or completed the vaccine series.

These recommendations have been proposed by the ACIP—a national group of experts that advises the Centers for Disease Control and Prevention (CDC) on vaccine issues. These recommendations are now being considered by CDC.

Why is the HPV vaccine recommended for such young girls?

Ideally, females should get the vaccine before they are sexually active. This is because the vaccine is most effective in girls/women who have *not* yet acquired any of the four HPV types covered by the vaccine. Girls/women who have not been infected with any of those four HPV types will get the full benefits of the vaccine.

Will sexually active females benefit from the vaccine?

Females who are sexually active may also benefit from the vaccine. But they may get less benefit from the vaccine since they may have already acquired one or more HPV type(s) covered by the vaccine. Few young women are infected with all four of these HPV types. So they would still get protection from those types they have not acquired. Currently, there is no test available to tell if a girl/woman has had any or all of these four HPV types.

Why is the HPV vaccine only recommended for girls/women ages 9 to 26?

The vaccine has been widely tested in 9-to-26 year-old girls/women. But research on the vaccine's safety and efficacy has only recently begun with women older than 26 years of age. The FDA will consider licensing the vaccine for these women when there is research to show that it is safe and effective for them.

What about vaccinating boys?

We do not yet know if the vaccine is effective in boys or men. It is possible that vaccinating males will have health benefits for them by preventing genital warts and rare cancers, such as penile and anal cancer. It is also possible that vaccinating boys/men will have indirect health benefits for girls/ women. Studies are now being done to find out if the vaccine works to prevent HPV infection and disease in males. When more information is available, this vaccine may be licensed and recommended for boys/men as well.

Studies have found the [HPV] vaccine to be almost 100% effective in preventing diseases caused by the four HPV types covered by the vaccine.

Should pregnant women get the vaccine?

The vaccine is not recommended for pregnant women. There has been limited research looking at vaccine safety for pregnant women and their unborn babies. So far, studies suggest that the vaccine has *not* caused health problems during pregnancy, nor has it caused health problems for the infant— but more research is still needed. For now, pregnant women should complete their pregnancy before getting the vaccine. If a woman finds out she is pregnant after she has started getting the vaccine series, she should complete her pregnancy before finishing the three-dose series.

Efficacy and Safety

Studies have found the vaccine to be almost 100% effective in preventing diseases caused by the four HPV types covered by the vaccine—including precancers of the cervix, vulva and vagina, and genital warts. The vaccine has mainly been studied in young women who had not been exposed to any of the four HPV types in the vaccine.

The vaccine was less effective in young women who had already been exposed to one of the HPV types covered by the vaccine.

This vaccine does not treat existing HPV infections, genital warts, precancers or cancers.

How long does vaccine protection last? Will a booster shot be needed?

The length of vaccine protection (immunity) is usually not known when a vaccine is first introduced. So far, studies have followed women for five years and found that women are still protected. More research is being done to find out how long protection will last, and if a booster vaccine is needed years later.

What does the vaccine not protect against?

Because the vaccine does not protect against *all* types of HPV, it will not prevent all cases of cervical cancer or genital warts. About 30% of cervical cancers will *not* be prevented by the vaccine, so it will be important for women to continue getting screened for cervical cancer (regular Pap tests). Also, the vaccine does *not* prevent about 10% of genital warts—nor will it prevent other sexually transmitted infections (STIs). So it will still be important for sexually active adults to reduce exposure to HPV and other STIs.

Will girls/women be protected against HPV and related diseases, even if they don't get all three doses?

It is not yet known how much protection girls/women would get from receiving only one or two doses of the vaccine. For this reason, it is very important that girls/women get *all three doses* of the vaccine.

The FDA has licensed the HPV vaccine as safe and effective. This vaccine has been tested in over 11,000 females (ages 9–26 years) around the world. These studies have shown no serious side effects. The most common side effect is soreness at the injection site. CDC, working with the FDA, will continue to monitor the safety of the vaccine after it is in general use.

Does this vaccine contain thimerosal or mercury?

No. There is no thimerosal or mercury in the HPV vaccine. It is made up of proteins from the outer coat of the virus (HPV). There is no infectious material in this vaccine.

Cost and Coverage of the HPV Vaccine

The retail price of the vaccine is $120 per dose ($360 for full series).

Will the HPV vaccine be covered by insurance plans?

While some insurance companies may cover the vaccine, others may not. Most large insurance plans usually cover the costs of recommended vaccines. However, there is often a short lag-time after a vaccine is recommended, before it is available and covered by health plans.

What kind of government programs may be available to cover HPV vaccine?

Federal health programs such as *Vaccines for Children* (VFC) will cover the HPV vaccine. The VFC program provides free vaccines to children and teens under 19 years of age, who are either uninsured, Medicaid-eligible, American Indian, or Alaska Native. There are over 45,000 sites that provide VFC vaccines, including hospitals, private clinics, and public clinics. The VFC Program also allows children and teens to get VFC vaccines through Federally Qualified Health Centers or Rural Health Centers, if their private health insurance does not cover the vaccine. For more information about the VFC, visit www.cdc.gov/nrp/vfc/Default.htm. Some states also provide free or low-cost vaccines at public health department clinics to people without health insurance coverage for vaccines.

Further Information on the Vaccine

The HPV vaccine is given through a series of three shots over a 6-month period. The second and third doses should be given 2 and 6 months (respectively) after the first dose.

Will girls/women who have been vaccinated still need cervical cancer screening?

Yes. There are three reasons why women will still need regular cervical cancer screening. First, the vaccine will NOT protect against all types of HPV that cause cervical cancer, so vaccinated women will still be at risk for some cancers. Second, some women may not get all required doses of the vaccine (or they may not get them at the right times), so they may not get the vaccine's full benefits. Third, women may not get the full benefit of the vaccine if they receive it after they've already acquired one of the four HPV types.

Should girls/women be screened before getting vaccinated?

No. Girls/women do not need to get an HPV test or Pap test to find out if they should get the vaccine. An HPV test or a Pap test can tell that a woman may have HPV, but these tests cannot tell the specific HPV type(s) that a woman has. Even girls/women with one HPV type could get protection from the other vaccine HPV types they have not yet acquired.

Will girls be required to get vaccinated before they enter school?

At least 50% of sexually active people will get HPV at some time in their lives.

There are no federal laws that require children or adolescents to get vaccinated. All school and daycare entry laws are state laws—so they vary from state to state. To find out what vaccines are needed for children or teens to enter school or daycare in your state, check with your state health department or board of education.

Facts About HPV and Cervical Cancer

Genital HPV is a common virus that is passed on through genital contact, most often during vaginal and anal sex. About 40 types of HPV can infect the genital areas of men and women. While most HPV types cause no symptoms and go away on their own, some types can cause cervical cancer in women. These types also have been linked to other less common genital cancers—including cancers of the anus, vagina, and vulva (area around the opening of the vagina). Other types of HPV can cause warts in the genital areas of men and women, called genital warts.

How is HPV related to cervical cancer?

Some types of HPV can infect a woman's cervix (lower part of the womb) and cause the cells to change. Most of the time, HPV goes away on its own. When HPV is gone, the cervix cells go back to normal. But sometimes, HPV does not go away. Instead, it lingers (persists) and continues to change the cells on a woman's cervix. These cell changes (or "precancers") can lead to cancer over time, if they are not treated.

How common is HPV?

At least 50% of sexually active people will get HPV at some time in their lives. Every year in the United States (U.S.), about 6.2 million people get HPV. HPV is most common in young women and men who are in their late teens and early 20s.

Anyone who has ever had genital contact with another person can get HPV. Both men and women can get it—and pass it on to their sex partners—without even realizing it.

How common is cervical cancer in the U.S.? How many women die from it?

The American Cancer Society estimates that in 2006, over 9,700 women will be diagnosed with cervical cancer and 3,700 women will die from this cancer in the U.S.

How common are genital warts?

About 1% of sexually active adults in the U.S. (about 1 million people) have visible genital warts at any point in time.

Is HPV the same thing as HIV or Herpes?

HPV is NOT the same as HIV or Herpes (Herpes simplex virus or HSV). While these are all viruses that can be sexually transmitted—HIV and HSV do not cause the same symptoms or health problems as HPV.

The only sure way to prevent HPV is to abstain from all sexual activity.

Can HPV and its associated diseases be treated?

There is no treatment for HPV. But there *are* treatments for the health problems that HPV can cause, such as genital warts, cervical cell changes, and cancers or the cervix, vulva, vagina and anus.

Other Ways to Prevent Cervical Cancer and HPV

Another HPV vaccine is in the final stages of clinical testing, but it is not yet licensed. This vaccine would protect against the two types of HPV that cause most (70%) cervical cancers.

Are there other ways to prevent cervical cancer?

Regular Pap tests and follow-up can prevent most, but not all, cases of cervical cancer. Pap tests can detect cell changes in the cervix *before* they turn into cancer. Pap tests can also detect most, but not all, cervical cancers at an early, curable stage. Most women diagnosed with cervical cancer in the U.S. have either never had a Pap test, or have not had a Pap test in the last 5 years.

There is also an HPV DNA test available for use with the Pap test, as part of cervical cancer screening. This test is used for women over 30 or for women who get an unclear (borderline) Pap test result. While this test can tell if a woman has HPV on her cervix, it cannot tell *which* types of HPV she has.

Are there other ways to prevent HPV?

The only sure way to prevent HPV is to abstain from all sexual activity. Sexually active adults can reduce their risk by being in a mutually faithful relationship with someone who has had no other or few sex partners, or by limiting their number of sex partners. But even persons with only one lifetime sex partner can get HPV, if their partner has had previous partners.

It is not known how much protection condoms provide against HPV, since areas that are not covered by a condom can be exposed to the virus. However, condoms may reduce the risk of genital warts and cervical cancer. They can also reduce the risk of HIV and some other STIs, when used all the time and the right way.

13

The HPV Vaccine Should Not Be Made Mandatory

Moira Gaul

Moira Gaul is a policy analyst for the Family Research Council, an organization that supports Christian family values.

In 2006 scientists formulated a vaccine that could protect women from becoming infected with human papillomavirus (HPV), a sexually transmitted disease that can cause cervical cancer. Although this vaccine is beneficial, it is also flawed in several ways and its use should not be mandatory in schools. The vaccine does not protect against all strains of HPV, including all of the strains that cause cervical cancer. Consequently, the government should not require that the vaccine be used in schools because doing so could send a dangerous message about safe sex.

My name is Moira Gaul. I have a master's of public health in maternal and child health from George Washington University, and I am working now as a policy analyst for the Family Research Council in Washington, D.C.

The Family Research Council welcomes the news that vaccines are in development for preventing infection with certain strains of the human papillomavirus (HPV). We also welcome the reports, like those we've heard this morning, of promising clinical trials for such a vaccine. Forms of primary prevention and medical advances in this area hold potential for helping

Moira Gaul, "Family Research Council Statement Regarding HPV Vaccines," Statement Given Before the Advisory Committee on Immunization Practices, Centers for Disease Control and Prevention, February 21, 2006. © 2006 by the Family Research Council. All rights reserved. Reproduced by permission of Family Research Council, 801 G Street, NW, Washington, DC 20001, 1-800-225-4008, www.frc.org.

to protect the health of millions of Americans and helping to preserve the lives of thousands of American women who currently die of cervical cancer each year as a result of HPV infection. Media reports suggesting that the Family Research Council opposes all development or distribution of such vaccines are false.

We are grateful to representatives of both Merck and GlaxoSmithKline for taking time to meet with us at the Family Research Council to explain their goals in developing these vaccines and their plans for the marketing and distribution of them. We will continue to take an interest in the process of determining whether such vaccines are safe and effective, and we are encouraged by the results so far. We will also continue to take an interest in the activities of the pharmaceutical companies, the federal and state governments, and of the medical community, as vaccines for HPV are approved, recommendations for their use are developed, and their use is implemented. In particular, we encourage follow-up studies to determine whether use of the vaccine has any impact on sexual behavior and its correlates, such as rates of other sexually transmitted diseases or rates of pregnancy.

The Limitations of the HPV Vaccine

We are particularly concerned with insuring that medically accurate information regarding the benefits and limitations of an HPV vaccine is distributed to public health officials, physicians, patients, and the parents of minor patients. It is especially important for those parties to understand that such a vaccine:

- will not prevent transmission of HIV or other sexually transmitted diseases, of which there are many;

- will not prevent infection with other strains of HPV, of which there are also many;

- will not prevent infection with all of the strains of HPV that cause cervical cancer;

- and lastly, will not eliminate the need for regular screening.

We recognize that the most current immunological studies suggest that these vaccines would be most effective in pre-adolescents. Our primary concern is with the message that would be delivered to nine- to twelve-year-olds with the administration of the vaccines. Care must be taken not to communicate that such an intervention makes all sex "safe." We strongly encourage the health care community to clearly communicate the medically accurate fact that only abstaining from sexual contact with infected individuals can fully protect someone from the wide range of sexually transmitted diseases.

Because the cancer-causing strains of HPV are not transmitted through casual contact, there is no justification for any vaccination mandate.

However, we also recognize that HPV infection can result from sexual abuse or assault, and that a person may marry someone still carrying the virus. These provide strong reasons why even someone practicing abstinence and fidelity may benefit from HPV vaccines.

The Vaccine Should Not Be Required

Because parents have an inherent right to be the primary educator and decision maker regarding their children's health, we would oppose any measures to legally require vaccination or to coerce parents into authorizing it. Because the cancer-causing strains of HPV are not transmitted through casual contact, there is no justification for any vaccination mandate as a condition of public school attendance. However, we do support the widespread distribution and use of vaccines against HPV.

Vaccination at the beginning of adolescence may provide a unique opportunity for both health care providers and parents to discuss with young people the full range of issues related to sexual health. We would encourage this committee to recommend that policy-making bodies, such as the American Academy of Pediatrics, should develop and formalize clinical counseling interventions directed toward sexual risk elimination strategies for pre-adolescents. Such strategies could be incorporated into anticipatory guidance protocols. Such a strategy would also mirror the risk elimination messages presented to adolescents regarding tobacco, alcohol, and drug usage, and youth violence prevention. This risk elimination message is the best form of primary prevention youth can receive.

Both health care providers and parents should reinforce the fact that limiting sexual activity to the context of one faithful and monogamous long-term relationship is the single most effective method of preventing all sexually transmitted diseases, unplanned pregnancies, and the whole range of negative psychological and social consequences that can result from sexual activity outside marriage.

Organizations to Contact

The editors have compiled the following list of organizations concerned with the issues debated in this book. The descriptions are derived from materials provided by the organizations. All have publications or information available for interested readers. The list was compiled on the date of publication of the present volume; the information provided here may change. Be aware that many organizations take several weeks or longer to respond to inquiries, so allow as much time as possible.

Alive and Well AIDS Alternatives
11684 Ventura Blvd., Studio City, CA   91604
(877) 411-AIDS • fax: (818) 780-7093
e-mail: info@aliveandwell.org
Web site: www.aliveandwell.org

Alive and Well AIDS Alternatives is an organization that presents information that questions the validity of many of the common assumptions about HIV and AIDS, including the accuracy of HIV tests and the effectiveness of AIDS drug treatments. The organization's Web site features information on whether a link exists between HIV and AIDS and also addresses facts and myths about AIDS drugs.

American Foundation for AIDS Research (AmFAR)
120 Wall St., 13th Fl., New York, NY   10005-3908
(212) 806-1600 • fax: (212) 806-1601
e-mail: information@amfar.org
Web site: www.amfar.org

AmFAR is a nonprofit organization that supports HIV/AIDS research, treatment education, and AIDS prevention. Its mission is to prevent HIV infection and to protect the human rights of everyone who is affected by the epidemic. The organization publishes a twice-yearly newsletter, a quarterly report on HIV/AIDS in Asia and the Pacific, an annual report, and several issue briefs.

American Social Health Association
PO Box 13827, Research Triangle Park, NC 27709
(919) 361-8400 • fax: (919) 361-8425
e-mail: info@ashastd.org
Web site: www.ashastd.org

The American Social Health Organization is a nonprofit organization that works to improve public health outcomes and is a leading authority on information pertaining to STDs. Facts and statistics about STDs are available on the Web site. The organization's publications include *HPV in Perspective* and *Managing Herpes*.

Canadian AIDS Society (CAS)
190 O'Connor St., Suite 800, Ottawa, ON K2P 2R3
   Canada
(613) 230-3580 • fax: (613) 563-4998
e-mail: casinfo@cdnaids.ca
Web site: www.cdnaids.ca

CAS is a national coalition of over 125 community-based AIDS organizations. The society is dedicated to improving the lives of people living with HIV/AIDS and strengthening Canada's response to the epidemic. CAS publishes position papers, including *HIV Vaccines*, fact sheets, and reports.

Centers for Disease Control and Prevention (CDC)—Sexually Transmitted Diseases
Mailstop E11, 1600 Clifton Rd., Atlanta, GA 30333
(800) 232-4636
Web site: www.cdc.gov/std

The CDC is one of the major components of the Department of Health and Human Services. Its purpose is to lead public health efforts to prevent and control the spread of infectious and chronic diseases. Its section on STDs provides information on various diseases, including fact sheets and statistics, as well as links to publications.

Concerned Women for America (CWA)

1015 Fifteenth St. NW, Suite 1100, Washington, DC   20005
(202) 488-7000 • fax: (202) 488-0806
Web site: www.cwfa.org

The CWA aims to promote biblical values throughout society in order to reverse the decline in America's moral values. CWA supports abstinence-only sexual education and questions the efficacy of condoms in preventing STDs. The organization publishes the magazine *Family Voice* and brochures, including "What Your Teacher Didn't Tell You About Abstinence."

Family Health International (FHI)

PO Box 13950, Research Triangle Park, NC   27709
(919) 544-7040 • fax: (919) 544-7261
Web site: www.fhi.org

The mission of FHI is to improve public health throughout the world through research and education. The organization works with research institutions, government organizations, and the private sector to achieve this goal. The FHI also aims to prevent the spread of STDs and provide care for people affected by those diseases. Books and reports are available on the Web site, including "Family Planning and the Prevention of Mother-to-Child Transmission of HIV."

Family Research Council (FRC)

801 G St. NW, Washington, DC   20001
(202) 393-2100 • fax: (202) 393-2134
Web site: www.frc.org

The FRC develops public policy that upholds the institutions of marriage and family; among the issues it supports is abstinence-only education. Publications on AIDS and abstinence-only education are available on the Web site, including "Why Wait: The Benefits of Abstinence Until Marriage."

Gay Men's Health Crisis (GMHC)
119 W. 24th St., New York, NY 10011
(212) 367-1000
Web site: www.gmhc.org

GMHC is an organization that helps lead the fight against AIDS. It aims to reduce the spread of HIV, improve the health and independence of people with HIV, and ensure that the prevention, treatment, and cure of HIV remains a national priority. The organization publishes fact sheets and the newsletter *Treatment Issues*. The Web site provides information on treatment, testing, and other STDs.

Guttmacher Institute
120 Wall St., 21st Floor, New York, NY 10005
(800) 355-0244 • fax: (212) 248-1951
e-mail: info@guttmacher.org
Web site: www.guttmacher.org

The mission of the institute is to use public education, policy analysis, and social science research to promote sound policy and create new ideas about sexual health. It aims to improve access to information about STDs. The organization publishes the periodicals *Perspectives on Sexual and Reproductive Health*, *International Family Planning Perspectives*, and *Guttmacher Policy Review*. The Web site features a section on STDs that includes fact sheets, policy briefs, articles, and reports, including *Adding It Up: The Benefits of Investing in Sexual and Reproductive Health Care*.

International AIDS Society (IAS)
Ch. de l'Avanchet 33, Cointrin, Geneva CH-1216
  Switzerland
+41-(0)22-7 100 800 • fax: +41-(0)22-7 100 899
e-mail: info@iasociety.org
Web site: www.iasociety.org

IAS is a worldwide independent association of HIV/AIDS professionals who are working to prevent, treat, and control the epidemic. The society organizes the International AIDS Conference. It publishes the journal *AIDS*, and the Web site links to articles about AIDS.

Sex Information and Educational Council of the United States (SIECUS)
130 W. 42nd St., Suite 350, New York, NY   10036-7802
(212) 819-9770 • fax: (212) 819-9776
e-mail: siecus@siecus.org
Web site: www.siecus.org

SIECUS is an organization that provides information for parents, health professionals, educators, and communities in order to ensure that everybody receives comprehensive information about sexuality. It also works to have sound public policy developed on sexuality-related issues. The council publishes the quarterly journal *SIECUS Report*, fact sheets, and newsletters.

World Health Organization (WHO)
Avenue Appia 20, Geneva 27   1211
   Switzerland
(+ 41 22) 791 21 11 • fax: (+ 41 22) 791 3111
e-mail: info@who.int
Web site: www.who.int

The World Health Organization is the United Nations specialized agency for health. The objective of WHO is to help all people achieve the highest possible level of health. The Web site has links to fact sheets and publications about HIV and AIDS, including "Taking Stock: HIV in Children" and "Sexual and Reproductive Health & HIV/AIDS".

Bibliography

Books

David Barlow, Ali Mears, and Dip Gum	*Sexually Transmitted Infections: The Facts.* Oxford: Oxford University Press, 2006.
Richard P. Barth	*Reducing the Risk: Building Skills to Prevent Pregnancy, STD & HIV.* Scotts Valley, CA: ETR Associates, 2004.
Garson J. Claton, ed.	*AIDS in Africa: A Pandemic on the Move.* New York: Novinka Books, 2006.
Jonathan Engel	*The Epidemic: A Global History of AIDS.* New York: Smithsonian Books/ Collins, 2006.
Emma Guest	*Children of AIDS: Africa's Orphan Crisis.* London: Pluto Press, 2001.
Michelle M. Houle	*AIDS in the 21st Century: What You Should Know.* Berkeley Heights, NJ: Enslow, 2003.
Miranda Hunter and William Hunter	*Staying Safe: A Teen's Guide to Sexually Transmitted Diseases.* Philadephia: Mason Crest, 2005.
Susan Hunter	*AIDS in America.* New York: Palgrave Macmillan, 2006.

Susan Hunter	*Black Death: AIDS in Africa*. Basingstoke, England: Palgrave Macmillan, 2003.
Sterling Lands	*Inside Out!: Character Development and Abstinence Education*. Austin: Greater Calvary, 2003.
Beryl Leach, Joan E. Paluzzi, and Paula Munderi	*Prescription for Healthy Development: Increasing Access to Medicines*. London: Earthscan, 2005.
Judith Levine	*Harmful to Minors: The Perils of Protecting Children from Sex*. Minneapolis: University of Minnesota Press, 2002.
Donald E. Morisky, ed.	*Overcoming AIDS: Lessons Learned from Uganda*. Greenwich, CT: Information Age Publishing, 2006.
Ann O'Leary, ed.	*Beyond Condoms: Alternative Approaches to HIV Prevention*. New York: Kluwer Academic, 2002.
Alvin Silverstein, Virginia Silverstein, and Laura Silverstein Nunn	*The STDs Update*. Berkeley Heights, NJ: Enslow Elementary, 2006.
M. Monica Sweeney and Rita Kirwan Grisman	*Condom Sense: A Guide to Sexual Survival in the New Millennium*. New York: Lantern Books, 2005.

Sabrina Weill   *The Real Truth About Teens & Sex:
                       From Hooking Up to Friends with
                       Benefits—What Teens Are Thinking,
                       Doing, and Talking About, and How
                       to Help Them Make Smart Choices.*
                       New York: Berkeley Publishing, 2005.

Diane Yancey   *STDs: What You Don't Know Can
                       Hurt You.* Brookfield, CT: Twenty-
                       First Century Books, 2002.

Periodicals

Lawrence K.   "Doctors Support a Childhood Vac-
Altman   cine for a Sex-Related Virus," *New
                       York Times*, October 28, 2005.

Lawrence K.   "Study Finds That Teenage Virginity
Altman   Pledges Are Rarely Kept," *New York
                       Times*, March 10, 2004.

Heather Boonstra   "Comprehensive Approach Needed to
                       Combat Sexually Transmitted Infec-
                       tions Among Youth," *Guttmacher Re-
                       port on Public Policy*, March 2004.

Jane E. Brody   "Abstinence-Only: Does It Work?"
                       New York Times, June 1, 2004.

Liz Conley   "We're Here, We're Queer: Get Used
                       to It," *SIECUS Report*, April–May
                       2003.

Wayne Ellwood   "We All Have AIDS: HIV/AIDS Is
                       Everyone's Problem," *New Interna-
                       tionalist*, June 2002.

Helen Epstein   "The Fidelity Fix," *New York Times Magazine*, June 13, 2004.

Kim Hak-Su   "Why We Must Defeat HIV/AIDS," *UN Chronicle*, March–May 2004.

B. Denise   "On the Frontline of the HIV/AIDS
Hawkins   Epidemic," *Black Issues in Higher Education*, March 24, 2005.

Todd Henneman   "Sex, Lies, and Teenagers," *Advocate*, August 16, 2005.

King K. Holmes,   "Effectiveness of Condoms in Pre-
Ruth Levine, and   venting Sexually Transmitted Infec-
Marcia Weaver   tions," *Bulletin of the World Health Organization*, June 2004.

Issues and   "Drug Patents and Developing Coun-
Controversies on   tries," March 28, 2003.
File

Claudia Kalb and   "Battling a Black Epidemic," *News-
Andrew Murr   week*, May 15, 2006.

Alison Katz   "AIDS in Africa," *Z Magazine*, September 2003.

Samantha Levine   "The Plague Busters," *U.S. News & World Report*, June 2, 2003.

Joseph Loconte   "The ABCs of AIDS," *Weekly Standard*, October 27, 2003.

Cory Richards   "Q: Should Congress Be Giving More Financial Support to Abstinence-Only Sex Education? No: Withholding Information About Contraception and Teaching Only Abstinence Puts Sexually Active Teens at Risk," *Insight on the News*, November 10, 2003.

Radhika Sarin   "The Feminization of AIDS," *Humanist*, January–February 2003.

Mpho Selemogo   "The African AIDS Crisis and International Indifference," *Humanist*, January–February 2006.

Judith Stephenson and Angela Obasi   "HIV Risk-Reduction in Adolescents," *Lancet*, April 10, 2004.

Patricia J. Sulak   "Adolescent Sexual Health," *Journal of Family Practice*, July 2004.

Todd Summers, Jennifer Kates, and Gillian Murphy   "The Global Impact of HIV/AIDS on Young People," *SIECUS Report*, October–November 2002.

Kathleen Tsubata   "Q: Should Congress Be Giving More Support to Abstinence-Only Sex Education? Yes: Abstinence Is Working to Decrease Teen Pregnancy and Is Building Among Our Nation's Youth," *Insight on the News*, November 10, 2003.

Claudia Wallis   "A Snapshot of Teen Sex," *Time*, February 7, 2005.

Kevin Whitelaw et al.   "In Death's Shadow," *U.S. News & World Report*, July 21, 2003.

World and I   "STDs: Yesterday and Today," March
                    2004.

Web Site

MedlinePlus: Sexually Transmitted Diseases
www.nlm.nih.gov/medlineplus/sexuallytransmitteddiseases
.html. This Web site, run by the U.S. National Library of
Medicine and the National Institutes of Health, provides
news and information on STDs. It also includes links to
research, statistics, and articles on diagnosis and prevention.

Index

India
  AIDS prevention efforts in, 45
Infertility
  in African society, 27–28
Intercourse
  anal/oral, prevalence of, 74
  condom use during, safety of,
    43
  heterosexual, HIV infections
    in women from, 13
  homosexual, dangers of,
    18–19

J

*Journal of Acquired Immune Defi-
ciency Syndrome,* 46
*Journal of Sexually Transmitted
Diseases,* 43

K

Kerry, John, 30
Kloser, Patricia, 50
Kral, Alex, 40, 41

M

McWalters, Peter, 68, 69
Media
  role in AIDS education, 65–66
  sex is promoted by, 16
Meeker, Meg, 16, 18
Methamphetamine
  is increasing HIV spread,
    37–42

N

National Center for Health Statis-
tics, 17
National Survey of Family
Growth, 75

Neisseria gonorrhoeae, 27
  See also Gonorrhea
New England Journal of Medicine,
48

O

Osten, Kevin, 39
Over, M., 24

P

Pap test, 84–85
Pelvic inflammatory disease (PID)
  costs of, in U.S., 28
  in developing world, 26–27
Pharmaceutical industry
  opposition of, to generic
    drugs, 55–56
Piot, P., 24
Planned Parenthood, 73–74
Poverty
  link between AIDS and, 56–57
  risk of HIV infection and, 32
Puberty
  in girls, average age for onset
    of, 16
Public health programs
  for HIV prevention, 40–41

S

Sexual activity
  among teens, methods to re-
    duce, 21–22
  is harmful to teenagers, 69–70
  outside of marriage, conse-
    quences of, 16–17, 21
Sexually transmitted diseases
(STDs)
  annual costs of, to U.S., 10, 14
  annual global incidents of, 24
  are international public health
    crisis, 23–28